keyboard

PRESENTS

STEAL
THIS
SOUND

PRESENTS

STEAL THIS SOUND

MITCHELL SIGMAN

Hal Leonard Books

An Imprint of Hal Leonard Corporation

Articles in this book originally appeared in *Keyboard* magazine, 2005–2011.

Published in cooperation with Music Player Network, New Bay Media, LLC, and *Keyboard* magazine. *Keyboard* magazine is a registered trademark of New Bay Media, LLC.

Published in 2011 by Hal Leonard Books
An Imprint of Hal Leonard Corporation
7777 West Bluemound Road
Milwaukee, WI 53213

Trade Book Division Editorial Offices
32 Plymouth Street, Montclair, NJ 07042

Printed in the United States of America

Book design by Damien Castaneda

Library of Congress Cataloging-in-Publication Data is available upon request.

ISBN 978-1-4234-9281-8

www.halleonardbooks.com

CONTENTS

INTRODUCTION

I'm willing to bet that many folks didn't take plug-in virtual synth instruments too seriously when they first appeared in Cubase DAW software circa 1999. I know I didn't—in my mind there was no way a rinky-dink little picture on a screen could make convincing synthesizer tones. I wasn't a Cubase user back then anyway, so they were irrelevant to me. But soon thereafter, all the big players were getting in on the virtual synth game, and once Emagic released the sophisticated ES2 virtual synth and EX24 sampler for Logic, I was hooked. With ES2, I had almost unlimited analog-style synthesis, while the EXS24 finally released me from the often hellish workflow of sample-edit-then-SCSI-dump to my Kurzweil K2000. Like many people, I quickly went from highly skeptical of virtual instruments to becoming a true believer. Most of my hardware digital synths and samplers were sold, or relegated to "live-show only" status.

These days, the sound quality and variety of available virtual instruments, as well as the relative affordability and power of modern CPUs, have made hardware digital instruments largely irrelevant. Some are still clutching their hardware workstations, and pure analog synths still have their own loyal following. But with portable hardware plug-in hosts and software such as Apple MainStage, others have gone 100 percent to plug-in virtual instruments, even in live settings.

I owe the genesis of this book to those very plug-ins I used to thumb my nose at. Back in 2004, I had an idea for a column where I would take a well-known track and detail how one could re-create its sounds using popular virtual synth plug-ins. I knew *Keyboard* magazine was the most appropriate outlet, but I had no connections in the magazine industry, and had never written professionally. What happened about one week later was truly one of the most serendipitous occurrences of my career.

A friend forwarded me an ad he found on Craigslist for pro LA-area keyboardists to participate in a roundtable forum that would last one hour; it paid $120. The ad didn't say much else, but it sounded to good me. On arrival about ten of us were shown into a boardroom. The host proceeded to ask questions about what we sought in a magazine for keyboardists. It soon became clear that we were participating in a focus group aimed at helping *Keyboard* magazine modernize its content and look. It was a nice exchange of ideas, and after the discussion it was revealed to us that *Keyboard*'s then-editor, Ernie Rideout, as well as art director, Janell Umemoto, were observing behind the one-way glass. Ernie joined us and graciously thanked everyone, and I knew this was my shot. I introduced myself and explained my column idea to Ernie. To my surprise, Ernie's response was, "That sounds great—write up a sample piece and send it to me!" I did, and though it took a few months before the pieces came together, I eventually had my own monthly column, initially titled *Vintage Sounds*.

I brainstormed a list of about a dozen ideas for articles at the outset. I figured once I exhausted those, I'd probably be out of ideas and *Keyboard* would be tired of me anyway. Six years later, I still have the privilege of being a monthly contributor, and now all the columns have been compiled here in this fine, leather-bound volume . . . er, paperback book.

I'd like to add a couple notes on the columns. You may notice that the earlier columns are longer than the later ones. This mostly had to do with changes in *Keyboard*'s editorial style as it evolved to include more graphics and less text (and maybe they grew tired of my incessant rambling!). Perhaps you'll find it a little easier to quickly create the sounds discussed in the more recent columns as there are more screen shots to guide you along.

The articles that appear here are as they appeared in the magazine. Please note that the text may include references to online links that may no longer be active and updates and changes to these sites may have occurred. That being said, YouTube is always a great resource (try searching the vintage synths mentioned in the text). Another great resource is www.vintagesynth.com; their reader forum is full of info pinpointing specific synths used in songs. And don't forget the entire www.keyboardmag.com site, which contains plenty of valuable information.

You'll also notice that I didn't write all the pieces. There were a couple months where *Keyboard* included some guest contributors to mix it up.

You'll see that there are a handful of virtual analog synths that I frequently use, but much of the time this isn't too important—most of the programming tricks described may be applied to almost any analog-style synth, be it virtual, inside, or outside a computer, or a real-deal analog synth. Most importantly, I hope this book makes you an all-around better programmer and helps you to quickly whip up any synth sound you need. Happy programming!

—MITCHELL SIGMAN
MARCH 2011

keyboard

PRESENTS

STEAL
THIS
SOUND

THE PROPHET SPEAKS

And the Analog Strings of Doom Sound

In an age where mega-gigabyte string-orchestra samples rule, many of us have forgotten the beauty of synthetic strings. The warmth and otherworldly swirl of these analog facsimiles gave '80s New Wave a shimmer all its own. Great examples abound in the music of early Duran Duran, Gary Numan, and my former employer, Berlin. How did these well-coiffed synthesists get their analog groove on?

During the '70s, the string synth of choice was the Solina String Ensemble, later to become the ARP String Ensemble—top-octave divide-down technology routed through a high-pass filter—a hybrid of organ and synth technology of the day.

But in the '80s, really fun analog string sounds came from the big bad polysynths, such as the Sequential Circuits Prophet-5 and the Moog Polymoog. I like to think of these two synths as the two main flavors of classic analog string sounds, each with their own unique tonality.

If you're lucky, you can give the following tips a try on a real Prophet or Polymoog. But the beauty of these beasts is that their sound can be accurately replicated using virtual analog synths, both hardware and software. I'm partial to Apple Logic ES2 and Native Instruments Pro-53. Whether you've got a software instrument, a virtual analog hardware synth, or the genuine article, let's dig in and twist some knobs.

PROPHET-5 PWM STRINGS

These tend to be of the dark and swirly variety, especially in the low-mid register; a great recorded example is Berlin's "Sex (I'm A)," which you can find on Berlin's *Best of Berlin*. The main characteristic of this sound lies in the use of pulse-width modulation (PWM). PWM refers to the use of an oscillator set to a square wave, but with the width or "duty cycle" constantly being made narrower or wider by a sweeping low-frequency oscillator (LFO). This gives the timbre constant movement, and also adds a bit of pitch modulation. All of this movement is great for approximating the constant shifting and beating of pitch inherent to a real string orchestra, albeit in a more synthetic fashion. The LFO waveform should be a triangle or sine wave. Make the depth as deep as possible without the oscillators shutting off at the extremes (when the waveform's pulse width gets too narrow, no sound is produced). I generally find the LFO speed should be pretty fast, but this is a matter of taste.

Use two oscillators for added thickness, or even more if you've got the horsepower. Set the initial pulse width setting on the oscillators a little differently on each for more variation. The idea is to have a bunch of oscillators swirling around, each at a slightly different rate. If your synth has a unison/poly mode that stacks extra oscillators but still allows you to play chords, this will make the sound even bigger. These frequently work in stereo; the ES2 implements this particularly well. The Pro-53 has an "analog" knob that messes with the pitch and filters a little and gives more life to sounds. Just don't go nuts, or the sound could become a little too messy!

The filter settings are pretty easy. Use a standard low-pass filter set to about 75 percent; no more open than that. Add a little bit of resonance to thin it out—we're not going for a huge pad.

Finally, the amplitude envelope is all about slow: slow attack, sustain set to hold forever, and long release. I usually set the attack as slow as possible for a song's tempo, but if it's too slow, you won't hear the beginnings of notes when quick melodies are played.

If you set everything right, the mid-to-upper keyboard range should be thick and undulating, and as you play lower notes, the sound will eventually become so murky and pitchy that it won't be usable, but that's what bass sounds are for, right? Have fun!

CLOCKWORK ORANGE (AND BLACK)

David Diamond's ARP 2600 Clockwork Patch

The ability to allow its hardwired connections to be overridden by patch cables gave the classic ARP 2600 huge flexibility. One of the sounds frequently identified with early ARP synths is the "percolating sequence"—a repetitive, rhythmic, sequenced pattern, usually driven from ARP's model 1601 sequencer (the 1601 was a 16-note sequencer capable of playing one 16-note pattern or two simultaneous 8-note patterns). Thanks to the Arturia 2600V and Way Out Ware TimewARP 2600 virtual synths, not only is the 2600 sound available again in an inexpensive and easy-to-find package, but the Arturia version features a neat re-creation of the 1601 sequencer.

One of the most recognizable "percolating sequences" is in the Who's "Baba O'Riley." Later on, the idea became a new wave mainstay—Vince Clarke of Erasure practically made a career out of these blippy sequence bits. My predecessor in Berlin, David Diamond, programmed a catchy pitched white-noise intro pattern on the band's 1984 hit, "No More Words." (I promise not to use any examples of my own band's music after this! I'm not getting any kickbacks.)

Instead of using the oscillators as sound sources, Dave used the white noise generator, fed through the filter section with the resonance turned up at least three quarters. This "cranked up" resonance causes the filter to ring—the internal feedback produces a pitched sine wave. When we set the filter cutoff frequency to track the keyboard, i.e., rise as the key played gets higher, this ringing sine wave can be played like a standard oscillator. For this example, I'm using the filter in band-pass mode, but the filter will "ring" in low-, band-, or high-pass modes too.

I used Arturia's fab 2600V plug-in to create this month's example, but the same patch could easily be created (albeit sans sequence) with the TimewARP 2600. Of course, anyone owning a real ARP 2600 and 1601 can do this too. And if you're one of those lucky few, I'm coming to, uh, "borrow" yours . . . forever!

First, let's set up our basic sound sources. You'll want to use the noise generator, and set the noise "color" slider all the way up so the noise generator outputs pure white noise—at lower settings, you get blue noise, an inherently darker timbre (as well as being a great band name).

Set the filter to band-pass mode. Set the cutoff frequency to around 1030 Hz and the resonance roughly three-quarters up (be careful when turning up the resonance to the point where it rings—it can get very loud unexpectedly and blow tweeters, ears, scare pets, etc. We know you're a musician and likely already deaf, but no need to sacrifice innocent bystanders . . .)

You'll want to set the amplitude envelope's controls to zero attack, decay all the way up, sustain at zero, and release around 1750 ms. Bring up the "Noise Gen" fader in the VCF section, and the VCF and LIN ADSR faders in the VCA section, and you should hear the noise when you play the keyboard. Right now our noise/ringing filter will only play one pitch, but we'll fix that.

Now we need to run some patch cables to and from the sequencer. First, connect the "Clocked Gate 1 Out" jack on the sequencer to the ADSR trigger "in" jack (it's the jack right below the big box that says ADSR) on the synth. This lets the sequencer trigger the envelope generator at every sequencer step. Now connect a cable from "Quantized Out A" on the sequencer to "KBD CV" in the VCF section on the synth. This does two things: It allows the sequencer slider controls to control the filter cutoff frequency, effectively playing our melody, and it allows the controller keyboard's relative voltage to transpose the pitches set by the sequencer sliders.

Now let's set our bus switches and voltage sliders in the sequencer. Rhythmically, this pattern is based on eighth-notes, with rests on the first eighth-note of each bar, so we'll set all the bus switches to "1," except the first switch on each set of eight, which can be set to "2." This will give us our eighth-note rests on the first beat of each bar.

We then need to set the voltage sliders to "play" the melody. The slider settings are as follows:

| 0 -12 0 +12 -12 +10 -12 +7 | 0 -12 0 -15 -12 0 -12 +7 |

This sends varying voltages to the filter cutoff frequency, changing the note the ringing filter produces and providing our percolating melody. Now would be a good time to set the sequencer's "Clock Freq" to around 4.5 Hz. If you're using a MIDI clock, the tempo is about 131 bpm.

Now we need a way for the keyboard to start and stop the sequence. We'll use the keyboard gate voltage; it's on when a key is held, off when the key is released. Patch a cable from the "Gate" jack beneath the AR section to the jack labeled "Start/Stop" on the sequencer. Now we can "play" the sequence. You may notice that every time you play a new note, the melody starts from where it left off when the last note was released. We can make it reset with every new note by patching a second cable from the "Gate" jack in the AR section to the jack labeled "Reset" on the sequencer. Now our melody plays from the top every time a new note is played.

This relatively simple "clockwork" patch should help you to get your head around the mysteries lurking within the 2600's powerful but sometimes intimidating semi-modular/patched sequencer environment.

"ON THE RUN" AND EMS FUN

Psychotic Bass Lines Are Yours for the Tweaking

APRIL 2005

This month I temporarily remove my New Wave hair hat and bounce backward into the pioneering era of analog synthesis. Back then, anyone adventurous enough (okay, it took money too) to embark on the purchase of one of these strange new devices was probably already well on the road to becoming a synth innovator!

One of the best known of these early innovators was Britain's Pink Floyd. Since being on the cutting edge of recording and sound technology was of the utmost importance to the Floyd, it's only natural that they were early embracers of analog synthesis technology. They were quirky Brits, at that, so it's fitting that the analog synths they embraced were the equally quirky EMS VCS3 and Synthi AKS analog synthesizers. EMS didn't have the notoriety of the Moog and ARP, but I suspect Floyd's choice had more to do with easy obtainability than English nationalism; Moogs and ARPs were pretty scarce in Blighty in those days, and FedEx service wasn't what it is today. Electronically speaking, the VCS3 and Synthi AKS were almost identical, but the VCS3 had form-factor and portability issues, eventually leading to the design of the Synthi A and Synthi AKS.

Perhaps the best-known demonstration of the humble little EMS synthesizers occurred on the *Dark Side of the Moon* track "On the Run." Here we'll re-create the throbbing bass sequence, which still sounds fantastic—a tribute to how far ahead of their time Pink Floyd truly were.

Pink Floyd used the integrated membrane keyboard/sequencer built into the Synthi AKS's suitcase lid. The bass sequence is just an eight-note repeating pattern, but the speed is so rapid that the individual notes aren't really audible. Instead they blend together, creating a distinctive whirling blur; a sort of audio pinwheel effect. The "On the Run" bass sound is a straightforward single-oscillator square wave routed straight into the voltage-controlled filter.

Though the Synthi's unique diode-ladder filter has a particular tonality, you should be able to get pretty close using most modern virtual analog synth plug-ins, as well as hardware synths. Start by setting a single oscillator to a square wave. If your synth offers a pulse width control, you'll want to set it to full width for as "square" a pulse width as possible, but most offer a fixed square wave. Disable any other oscillators by turning them off or all the way down in the oscillator mix section.

If you have the option, set the filter slope parameter to 12 dB or 18 dB per octave, letting a little more high-end through than a more common 24-dB-per-octave filter (though the VCS3 and Synthi filters are often listed as having an 18-dB-per-octave slope, the filter is reported to have a slope that varies considerably dependent upon its settings. Ahh, you quirky Brits!). The filter should initially be set about three-quarters of the way open, with resonance about halfway up. Clearly the Floyds were constantly playing with the cutoff and resonance controls as the song progressed, so by all means, go nuts! You'll want to set the filter envelope with quick attack and decay times.

The sustain and release settings won't really matter because the notes move so quickly, so keep these at zero.

The amplitude envelope will be of the "gate" variety (i.e., attack on zero, decay on zero, sustain full up, and release on zero). You might want to set your synth to mono retrigger mode instead of the standard poly mode. This way, you'll be sure to get the "one-note-at-a-time" old-school monosynth effect from the sequence. This brings us to the fun part—the sequence itself!

The sequence was originally programmed on the Synthi AKS's minimal built-in sequencer. Unless you're using a virtual synth with a built-in sequencer (such as Arturia's Moog Modular V or ARP 2600V), you'll probably just program the notes using a standard computer sequencer such as Cubase, Logic, or any other equivalent. Reason's Matrix sequencer would be perfect for this too. The notes will be in the bass register, and are as follows:

Program these as sixteenth notes, crank the tempo up to 166 bpm, begin twirling those filter knobs, and you're off! To make things a little spicier and spacier, add some bus reverb as well. I used Logic Pro's "Big and Warm Plate" preset in the Space Designer plug-in to great effect. A little simulated tape delay would be wicked too.

Triggering mid-tempo repeating sixteenth notes at a different tempo and panning them randomly will help achieve the "helicopter diving in dangerously close" effect, heard at 1:49. Adding a guitarist with bagful of feedback effects will help your cause as well, especially if you record the feedback and reverse it.

For most impressive effect, be sure to dim the lights, crank the lava lamp up to full goo, and laugh randomly like a lunatic. You'll know you're on track when you start hearing voices in your head and the men come to lock you up!

You too can go to the dark side of the moon with Propellerhead Reason; here we've put the sequence into a Matrix module (transposed to C minor from E minor), and called up a square wave patch on Subtractor.

POWER OF ONE

Making Lots of Sound with Just a Single-Oscillator Patch

One of the benefits of today's massively powerful computers and synths is the tremendous amount of sonic horsepower emanating from scads of stacked oscillators grinding away. Many musicians turn up their noses at instruments that don't offer cubic polyphony and stackability, allowing huge, detuned walls of sonic doom. But they're missing out.

Not so long ago, two-oscillator-per-voice polysynths were all there were, and instruments like the Moog Micromoog and the ARP Axxe only contained one oscillator. Banish the thought!

How did keyboardists get by with just one measly oscillator? Could you even make a decent noise? You bet! When you consider it, the vast majority of acoustic instruments are single-oscillator instruments. But despite their "monotonic" nature, they manage to be expressive and interesting. This is usually the result of clever manipulation of pitch and amplitude, in the form of vibrato and tremolo, as well as expressive phrasing.

The idea here is simple: Though a single-oscillator synth patch can often sound thin and unimpressive on its own, often times it will fit better in the mix than a large, furry, multi-oscillator monster. Imagine a band where every instrument sounded as big as the philharmonic string section and you'll get the idea.

My favorite of the single-oscillator squawks came from Greg Hawkes of the Cars. Starting back in '78 with the band's eponymous debut, Hawkes always seemed to wring sounds from his synths that were the opposite of the big Moog bass sweeps so fashionable then. Instead he frequently favored a simple single-oscillator synth lead that cut right through the Cars' muscular dual-guitar attack. You can hear lots of examples on the first two Cars albums, *The Cars* and *Candy-O*.

This sound mostly emanated from a MiniKorg 700s, a rather funky little monosynth from the early '70s that predated the big-guns polysynths of the late '70s and '80s (you can check out Greg furiously whacking away at the switches protruding from the MiniKorg's front edge in the great *The Cars Live—Musikladen* 1979 DVD).

So with no further ado, here's the simple recipe for getting these sounds nailed from a virtual analog soft or hardware synth. In the oscillator section, select—you guessed it—one oscillator using a sawtooth wave. The filter should be of the low-pass variety. Try to resist the urge to crank it wide open; real instruments usually aren't this bright. Besides, if you want to tweak it while you're playing, this will give you somewhere to go. A little resonance will also help it sound more organic, although it's not necessary. We don't really need any filter envelope as this simple sound will basically stay the same through its duration. The amp envelope should be a super-simple on/off affair: quick attack, quick release.

Here's where the secret sauce comes into play. To avoid a totally static "test tone" sound, add some vibrato courtesy of an LFO. We want to route the LFO to modulate the pitch of the oscillator, and set the waveform to a triangle or sine wave shape. Take extra time to get the speed and depth settings just right; we want a medium speed with around a quarter-tone of depth. You should be able to feel when it has just the right amount of wobble to it.

The other lifesaver for single-oscillator patches is portamento, also known as "glide." Set this carefully, as setting it too fast tends to minimize the effect, and making it too slow can make the pitches come out improperly as you play a melody. But sometimes a fast setting works to add just a touch of character, as in the verse melodies of the Cars' "Just What I Needed."

Finally, you may want to experiment with effects, as a subtle delay can always help a single-note line, and chorus can be interesting as well. Chorus on a single oscillator has a different character than simply detuning a second oscillator; this largely became the signature sound of Roland's highly successful Juno series of synthesizers.

Next time you're ready to whip out a heavy-hitting lead tone, try cutting down, save that computer horsepower, and see why one isn't the loneliest number!

The hardest thing about creating great single-oscillator patches is resisting the urge to engage additional oscillators. In Apple's Logic Pro, you can easily make with the patch described using the ES2 soft synth. Here's what that patch looks like.

CAN I GET A BLING-BLING?

Cast a Spell with Triangle Wave Bells

When most people think of the golden age of analog synthesis, the first sound that springs to mind is usually that of huge and fat oscillators chewing away and moving lots of air in the room. These are the classic sounds that shook the rump of the world. But on the flip side of the frequency spectrum lives a whole other set of sounds, those of delicate high-register tinkles.

Throughout the '70s, the Fender Rhodes electric piano was the de rigueur choice for any bell-like keyboard sound. But by the '80s, polysynths ruled the roost, and analog synths were employed for all manner of blings and dings to fill out a mix. This lasted until samplers and the ubiquitous Yamaha DX7 changed synthesized bell sounds forever.

Today it seems virtual analog synths are used in a much more limited way than their real counterparts a couple of decades ago. Now most percussive synth noises are doled out to a ROM-based sampler or an FM synth. But a great alternative for interesting high-register synth sounds is to utilize the oft-ignored triangle waveform to create what I call the "octave triangle pling" sound (they don't pay me to come up with catchy names!). This sound opens the door to experimentation with more "blingy" sounds, as I like to refer to them. They don't really sound like bells, but they sound great anyway!

Before we get into the serious knob twirling, let's cite some examples. Howard Jones used the "triangle bling" in the verses of his track "Pearl in the Shell" from the *Human's Lib* record, likely emanating from a Roland Jupiter-8. Vince Clarke used it not only in Depeche Mode's classic "Just Can't Get Enough" but also on several tracks of Yaz's *Upstairs at Eric's*. Listen to "Goodbye Seventies" at 1:42 for a perfect example. The Human League used this sound in a slightly lower register at 3:43 in the keyboard solo of their track "Do or Die" from the amazing *Dare* album. And you can also hear it in the verses of Berlin's "Pictures of You" from their album *Love Life*. This was originally performed on a Sequential Circuits Prophet-5, but I play it live on an Alesis Ion. Here's how to do it!

The main ingredients of this sound are the oscillator settings. Start with a sawtooth wave on the first oscillator. On the second oscillator, set it to a triangle but transpose it up one octave higher. Then detune the triangle oscillator a bit for a chorusing effect; I find about 10 cents to be good. You'll also want to apply some vibrato from an LFO. One of my favorite analog tricks is to apply a slow vibrato to one oscillator only in a two-oscillator patch. This sounds a little more musical than just applying the vibrato equally to both, as their pitch relationship will always be changing a little, as opposed to both pitches moving up and down together in lockstep. If you have three oscillators available, you can add another triangle wave in the same octave as the second oscillator, but this time, detune the pitch the other direction (if the second oscillator is detuned +10 cents, then set the detuning to −10 on oscillator three). You can apply some of the vibrato as well, but at a slightly different depth to keep things interesting. Timbrally speaking, we now have a pretty rich sound.

You don't really need to use the filters at all, as standard low-pass filters will dull your "bling." But you can optionally set the filter in high-pass mode and trim out some bottom end. In addition to simply removing low frequencies, high-pass filters tend to impart a delicate, crystalline quality, which will likely help our "blinginess" (I bet there's a nasty editor's note about me making up words by the time you read this!). [Keep it moving, Mitchell. —Ed.] Consider the high-pass filter optional, though, as the "no filter" version still sounds great.

In the amp/envelope section, set the envelope for instant attack, a relatively long decay, no sustain, and a relatively long release—we want to mimic a guitar or piano type of envelope. Make sure there's plenty of release, as this sound was born to play cascading arpeggios and scales. And if you have the option, set the polyphony pretty high so that the tails of notes don't get cut off.

That's all you need. You may want to try some delay or reverb, but this sound seems to work pretty well on its own. The detuned oscillators give sort of a chorusing effect and the long release lends a faux reverb effect. You know you've done well in the analog realm when you finish programming a sound and it stands up without tons of effects. Have fun making the bling-bling sing.

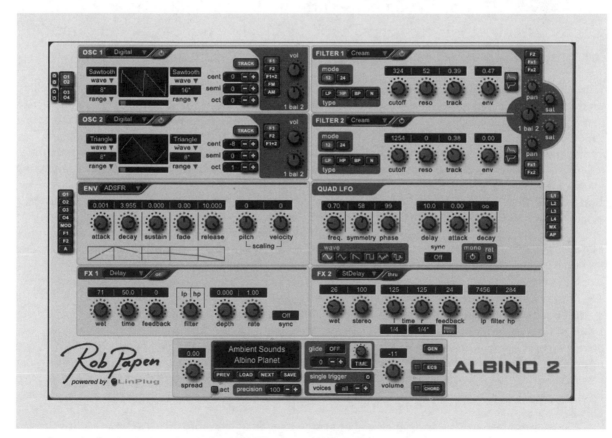

Here are the basic settings for a classic "bling" sound, using LinPlug Albino 2. Note that osc 3, osc 4, filter 2, and FX2 have been disabled. This sound may be simple, but it's got quite a discography.

Creating Analog Polysynth Organs

AUGUST 2005

The mighty organ has been a staple of rock, pop, and jazz for, well, a really long time. The original Hammonds were heavy, unwieldy beasts, so there have been many attempts at packing those big sounds into more portable packages. With the advent of analog polysynths in the late '70s and early '80s, organ tones—and their sine wave building blocks—were a natural candidate for imitation.

Virtually every analog polysynth of that era, including the Prophet-5, Oberheim OB-X series, and Roland Juno and Jupiter series, offered organ emulations with varying degrees of accuracy. But as often happens in analog synthesis, the relative lack of realism in these re-creations made for new and interesting sounds.

To get their sound, organs use what is essentially additive synthesis, in which many simple tones are added together to create a complex tone. This dates back to the days of pipe organs employing many pipes in varying octaves, with different pipes offering different tonal characteristics. This tradition continued with the classic Hammond tone wheel organs, with spinning toothed wheels suspended in a magnetic pickup field replacing the pipe organ's large pipes.

Conversely, analog subtractive synthesis works in reverse. Instead of adding numerous simple tones together to generate rich harmonics, subtractive synthesis begins with one or two oscillators generating harmonically rich tones, running through a filter that removes harmonics.

To re-create this reverse engineering process, let's start with the oscillator section. Either a sawtooth or a fixed pulse waveform will work. If you choose a pulse wave, you'll want to set the pulse width to a medium setting; too wide will make it too flutey, and too narrow will sound too brash and thin. If your synth has a sub-oscillator, turn it up. If you have a second oscillator, use it as well, preferably set one octave up or down from oscillator one, and detuned by four to ten cents. The idea here is to have a couple of different tone sources working in separate octaves. You can even use a third oscillator with similar settings, but detune it in the opposite direction of the second one for more of a chorusing effect. You can also use a low frequency oscillator (LFO) to apply vibrato to the oscillators. Make sure to pitch-modulate all oscillators equally.

If your synth allows you to set the number of simultaneously playable notes, set it to eight voices or more so you can play the kind of two-fisted chords often heard in organ styles.

Filter settings will vary depending on how bright you want your organ to be, but try to resist the urge to crank it wide open. This will help make your tone sound less like a synth and more like an organ. We won't be varying the filter settings with any envelope modulation, since organ sounds are typically static.

Be sure to experiment with resonance settings, though, as this imparts a warm mid-range tone that will sound more organ-like and less hi-fi and synthetic.

The amplitude envelope is as simple as it gets: fast attack and decay, full sustain and quick release; essentially, you're creating an on/off switch.

As a finishing touch, try adding some deep chorus or a phaser effect to approximate a Leslie rotating speaker. This can be a really important ingredient in obtaining convincing organ-isms. The single-oscillator Roland Juno synths really came to life just using its built-in chorus.

Now go fill in those pads and riffs with swanky synth organ tones!

Dial up an organ on your fave synth—here's the organ patch on McDSP's Synth One.

I LIKE THE WAY YOU WERK IT

Mad Arpeggios from Hyperspace with Kraftwerk

Kraftwerk is arguably the most influential group in electro history. During a relatively short period in the '70s, Kraftwerk released the innovative "holy trinity" of electronic pop, *Trans-Europe Express*, *The Man-Machine*, and *Computer World*. And years later, they're still on top of their, uh, computer game with a successful tour and a live "greatest hits" compilation entitled *Minimum Maximum* (clever, guys!).

Perhaps the most innovative aspect of the early Kraftwerk records was their pioneering use of sequencers. In the early '70s, sequencers were certainly not the ubiquitous software items they are today; they were mostly constructed from unobtainium, and most keyboardists didn't really understand how they could be utilized. As a result, most were stunned by the rigid, perfectly executed patterns created on these recordings, and likely imagined banks of exotic custom computers behind the scenes, operated by droids. Surely this was Kraftwerk's intention, as they went out of their way to shroud almost all aspects of their creation in mystery. This is evident in their albums' almost complete lack of liner notes and the near-identical physical appearance of the band members. Their secrecy also shows in their rather vague answers when questioned about their studio and the instruments used to create their music (see Jim Aikin's May '82 interview, reprinted in *Keyboard*'s excellent *The Best of the '80s* book).

In reality, it's likely that Kraftwerk was using nothing more than standard Moog modular synths and other popular analog monosynths of the day. Most of the sequenced passages are simple, repeated patterns, which could easily have been produced using either the Moog modular's 960 sequencer or an ARP sequencer. These devices were pretty crude compared to today's sequencer apps. Most offered a row of 8 or 16 knobs or sliders, each of which was set to output a corresponding voltage. This generally was routed to control pitch, but could also control a filter, or any other voltage-controllable parameter, resulting in a repeating pattern. Analog sequencers also contained a built-in clock, which was simply used to regulate tempo, but the clock itself could be voltage-controlled using LFOs or other sources. Things could get crazy pretty quick on a modular synth!

The track we'll be examining this month is "Home Computer" from the *Computer World* record. At 1:37, you'll hear a dreamy and atonal 16-note passage. To re-create this otherworldly sequence, we can use a modeling synth with a built-in sequencer (such as the ones featured in Arturia's Moog Modular V and ARP 2600V, or Korg's MS2000 hardware synth). As a simpler alternative, we can just create the basic sound and program the actual notes into standard music-sequencing software, such as Cubase or Logic. This is the approach we'll take here, but if you're adventurous, you can make the sound "self-contained" by programming the notes into a virtual analog with a built-in sequencer.

The basic sound source here is not a standard voltage-controlled oscillator. Instead it is the sound of a voltage-controlled filter with its resonance turned up to the point of oscillation (much like the Joe Walsh "Life's Been Good" sequencer patch described later). This gives a distinctive, ringing, pure sine-wave tonality. You'll want to start by actually turning off the synth's oscillators. Turn up filter resonance (sometimes called "emphasis") all the way. Some virtuals, such as Logic's ES2 (which I used to create this patch), have a "filter reset" parameter that you can use to make the filter oscillation trigger more consistently, or else you can turn up the white noise a little in your synth's mixer. Either way, having some actual sound going into the filter "excites" the ringing that makes it oscillate. You may or may not need it, depending on your soft synth.

Make sure the filter is in low-pass mode, and set its keyboard tracking control so that the keyboard plays a standard chromatic scale. This is usually the "full up" setting on the keyboard tracking control or switch (on the ES2, it's 0.51). Make sure the filter envelope knob is all way down, or else the pitches will swoop wildly.

We want to set the amplitude envelope to a medium-fast attack, just slow enough so that the start of a note doesn't click. Decay should be medium (about 100 ms), and sustain and release can be all the way down.

The sequence consists of sixteenth notes at about 121 bpm. Here are the notes:

| B C# B C# | D# F# A B | C D# F F# | G G# B D |

Amusingly, the notes are somewhat approximate, because the analog sequencer used on the original track didn't quantize its output to half steps, so some of the notes are slightly "between" pitches. In other words, the pot used to set each step simply would set voltage in a linear fashion instead of stepping through notes. This leads me to believe that Kraftwerk used a Moog or home-brew sequencer, because ARP's 1601 sequencer featured voltage quantization for accurately setting notes to musically correct half steps.

Add an eighth-note tempo-synced delay (about 248 ms) with around 40 percent feedback. Some reverb wouldn't hurt our cause either; I like the Moog spring reverb emulation in Logic's Space Designer. Delay and 'verb really go a long way toward giving these types of sequences personality!

And that's it—into the mysterious world of kraut space we go. You can try similar tricks to re-create the intro of Kraftwerk's "Spacelab" from *The Man-Machine.* This is basically sixteen ascending notes of a whole-tone scale, with a sequencer speeding up to oblivion (and a whole bunch of echo).

Have fun doing a little robot dance—Klaus Nomi would be pleased!

Here's what the patch looks like on Arturia's Minimoog V.

ARM THE LASERS!

Hit Me (Hit Me!) with Those Laser Beams

OCTOBER 2005

If you're like me (and one hopes you aren't), you know that the most fun thing to do with a synth is to make crazy sounds that drive your friends and family nuts. So this month, instead of the musical vintage synth sounds we usually explore, we will discuss the sound effect analog synths were born to make: the mighty laser!

Of course, we all know that in reality lasers don't make any sound at all, but as far as the Sci-Fi Channel is concerned, they make a heck of a racket. Getting back to that music thing we do, laser swoops tend to be really good for segues or as intros and outros to different musical sections. "Give us some examples!" you say. How about Madonna's "Ray of Light?" Courtesy of William Orbit's skilled Korg MS-20 wrangling, the *thips* come thick. The Human League's *Dare* album has them in abundance. Check out "Sound of the Crowd." And Trans-X's '80s synth-trash chestnut "Living on Video" has enough lasers to blow up the Death Star.

There are myriad ways to create laser swoops and blasts in the analog realm, but for your convenience I've divided them into two separate categories. The first category is the "swept oscillating filter" variety. It's really just a variation of the classic rez-zap effect used in dance music, but with the speed of the sweep slowed down. These are neat, but the real mayhem lies in the type I'll explain next: the FM modulated-sweep laser.

Instead of using the filter as a sound source, we use a standard oscillator, but it will be modulated by another oscillator in the audio range. Holy carrier frequency, Batman, what does that mean!? What we're going to do is a very basic version of FM synthesis (made famous by the Yamaha DX7).

Here's what's going on. FM, or "frequency modulation," synthesis is just a complex way of saying that we're taking an oscillator and using it to create sound, and then using a second oscillator to create a vibrato by "modulating" the pitch of the first one, usually at a very slow rate of a couple cycles per second. This is why you can hear vibrato undulating up and down. The secret of FM synthesis is that the speed of this vibrato is very fast, way too fast to hear it going up and down. This has the effect of "bending" the waveform of the oscillator outputting the sound in strange and often extreme ways. Combine a bunch of these pairs of sound source and modulating oscillators in different configurations, and you have a DX7 (and clichéd but cool '80s clanky bass sounds, but that's another month's column).

Getting back to our lasers, here's how we can use this idea in the world of analog to make kick-butt lasers. Keep in mind that you'll need a synth that has the capability to modulate one oscillator with the other to do it. Native Instruments' Pro-53 and Arturia's Minimoog do, as well as the Alesis Ion/Micron, Nord Lead, and Korg MS2000/MicroKorg.

Set oscillator one to a sine or triangle wave, and turn its level up in the mixer section. Turn oscillator two all the way down. This is the potentially tricky part. Basically, you'll need to determine how to route the second oscillator so that its pitch modulates the first oscillator. This is sometimes referred to as "cross modulation." Depending on the synth, this can be really easy (like on the Nord Lead, which has an FM knob), or a little less obvious (Prophet-5s and their virtual cousins accomplish this with the "poly-mod" section). You can try all the different oscillator waves for different flavors, but sine or triangle waves usually sound nicest.

Once you get this "cross-mod" going, you'll want to use envelope two to sweep the frequency of oscillator one. In other words, we want the pitch of the first oscillator to go up and down slowly via the envelope, resulting in our laser swoop. As in our other example, you'll want to route envelope two to the first oscillator, and set the attack pretty quick and the decay long. Set the amp envelope to "on/off" and off you go.

If your synth has an oscillator unison mode, turn it on to increase the size of the blast! Be sure to throw some chorus and/or delay on it as well. Now blast away—Dr. Evil would be proud!

BIG BOTTOM DRIVES ME OUT OF MY MIND

The Moog Bass Tones That Rumbled the Earth

NOVEMBER 2005

This month we close down the VCA for a moment of silence and honor the passing of the father of modern-day analog synthesis, Dr. Robert Moog. There's probably not much I can say in this space that hasn't already been said elsewhere, but here goes. As I kid, I remember the wonder of seeing a fisheye-lens photo of Roger Powell manipulating a Moog, with a serious and stoic-looking Bob behind him as control commander. I was hooked. Luckily, my supportive parents helped me secure a Realistic MG-1 (basically a Moog Rogue with a few control changes) at the age of 12 and I've never looked back.

It's only fitting that we honor Bob by exploring what might be the Minimoog's most important contribution to the pop music lexicon: the righteously fat and funky Minimoog bass sound. Let's get into making some badass bass noise, shall we?

There are a couple of defining factors in what makes the Moog bass sound unique. The first is Bob's patented "ladder" filter. Without getting too techy, it makes for a bold, "fat" sound that really separates the Mini from other synths. The second is the behavior of the envelopes—snappy attack and "legato"; when you strike a key, the filter/amplitude envelopes are triggered. If you strike a second key without lifting the first, the envelope doesn't retrigger. This can be really expressive with a long envelope, as notes tend to gracefully add on to a phrase until you lift all fingers and start again. This is how funkmeister Bernie Worrell made those growly high-speed wipes up and down the keyboard (try it!). The third factor is the subtle overdrive that often occurs in the Minimoog's circuits, which tends to round off and fatten the Mini's tonality.

If you're in the plug-in world, the no-brainer go-to synth would be Arturia's Minimoog V, which is good enough that Bob Moog himself gave it his stamp of approval. In the hardware realm, there's the Minimoog Voyager and Little Phatty, as well as the Studio Electronics SE-1, which are real-deal analog synths. For those on a tighter budget, the Alesis Ion/Micron series has three oscillators and a pretty nicely modeled Moog filter. If you don't have access to any of these, you may still be able to get close by setting up the patch described, and then adding some subtle compression and/or overdrive. But go easy, grasshopper. We want subtle coloration, not metal meltdown.

Whatever synth you're using, you'll want to start with two—preferably three—oscillators, all set to sawtooth waves. You can try square waves as well, but we'll stick with saws for this example. You'll want to tune the oscillators in octaves; if you have three, set two of them to the same octave and one of them up one octave. Detune ever so slightly, but keep them pretty close. This "almost in tune" sound helps capture the Moog vibe (though some go the other way and detune like crazy).

Filter settings can vary, but for this example we're going to go with a pretty resonant sound, so we'll turn the cutoff down to about 30 percent (about 10 o'clock), and the resonance up to about 70 percent (or 3 o'clock). We want just a little envelope control of the filter, say about 15 percent (5:30 or 6 o'clock). And the filter envelope should have a quick, but not instant, attack, say about 200 ms. Decay will be around 600 ms, and sustain level is low.

Our amplitude envelope should have an instant-on attack, about 300 ms decay, and the sustain level full up.

For flavor, add some glide, but just a little so you can hear quick little sweeps between notes. Effects-wise, you can add compression to make it pop more, or a little warm overdrive, but not much else; any time-based effects will dilute the in-your-face factor.

Now you're knee-deep in the funk. And may Dr. Robert A. Moog rest in peace.

Here's what this month's sound looks like on the front panel of Arturia's Minimoog V soft synth—it would look about identical on a real Mini. Newbies should note that in Mini nomenclature, filter resonance is called "emphasis," and the terminology is faithfully reproduced on Arturia's simulation. Don't let it throw you; most other synths (real and virtual) call it "resonance."

DOMO ORIGATO, MR. OSTINATO

Ostinati Are Anything but Ostentatious

Our friends at dictionary.com define "ostinato" as "a short melody or pattern that is constantly repeated, usually in the same part at the same pitch" (sounds like my entire career as a professional keyboardist . . .) In other words, the same note, over and over. On paper, it sounds useless, but in the world of synth pop, ostinati can serve a nifty dual purpose; they provide the rhythmic pulse of a percussion track, but since they're pitched notes, they reinforce the harmonic structure of the song. Which is especially important when four inept British guys are all playing the same note with one finger.

A number of classic synth bands have used sixteenth-note ostinatos to rhythmically propel tracks. These include the often-overlooked Japan, on tracks such as "Gentlemen Take Polaroids" (as well as many of the others from the album of the same name), Duran Duran's "Hold Back the Rain," and New Order's "Perfect Kiss." Although these sequencey synth bits were out of vogue for a while, the "new" New Wave appears to be bringing them back. Listen to the Bravery's "An Honest Mistake" for an obvious nod to New Order.

There are a number of ways to approach creating your own percolating ostinatos. In the pre-MIDI '80s, most acts were using basic hardware sequencers and hoping the drummer could keep up (or tearing their hair out trying to make the drum machine sync properly). These days, you can easily program a single-note "blip" and simply play all the notes individually in a sequencer. But it's more fun to create patches with the triggering and basic note patterns built into the sound.

Let's delve into re-creating the "osti" figure from Duran Duran's "Hold Back the Rain" from their '82 release, *Rio* (and when we're done here, I'll auction off my collection of Nagel paintings that I swiped from Don Johnson's house). What we have here is a thick, moving pulse-width modulation sound playing two notes each of an up-and-down octave pattern.

First, set two or three oscillators to the pulse-wave position. You'll want to set one of them an octave down, and then detune the others by a couple of cents to make 'em fat. Now we want to invoke some classic, constantly shifting pulse-width modulation. This way the waveform is constantly in motion, making our basic timbre a little more interesting. We'll do this by routing a slow-moving LFO set to a sine or triangle wave to the oscillators' pulse width parameter. Sometimes this is referred to as "shape," or in the case of MOTU's MX4 virtual analog synth, which I'm using for this month's demonstration, "symmetry." You can also vary the initial pulse-width setting for each oscillator a bit to further differentiate the tones.

We really don't need any filter at all; we want full-blast high end, so just bypass the filter. If that's not an option, just select a low-pass filter and turn the cutoff all the way up.

The amplitude envelope should be set with instant attack and a relatively quick decay. You may need to experiment with it once the notes are playing. Release should be quick as well.

This should get us going on the basic sound. Depending on the synth you've used, you can get your ostinato pattern going a number of ways. If you're fortunate enough to be using MOTU's MX4, you can jump over to the "mods" page, which contains all matter of arpeggio and triggering sources. Just set the pattern gate to sixteenth notes and the arpeggiator to eighth notes, then hold down an octave in the key of E and you're there—two high notes, two low ones.

If you're using a synth that doesn't have any sort of built-in arpeggiator or auto note triggering, here's a neat way to fake it: In the amp section, set the envelope for a standard "on/off" type envelope, i.e., attack zero, decay zero, sustain full, release zero. Then route a LFO set to a sawtooth wave to the amp, or VCA. Set the LFO speed to the tempo of the sixteenth notes and play eighth notes in octaves. The most important thing here is that the LFO saw wave must start at the top and fall; otherwise, your sound will keep fading up at the LFO rate, losing its punchy attack. As an alternative, you can apply this trick to the filter instead of the amp for a different sound; just make sure you start with the cutoff frequency all the way down.

Be sure to bomb the whole thing in lots of swirling chorus, and like Prince says, there is joy in repetition!

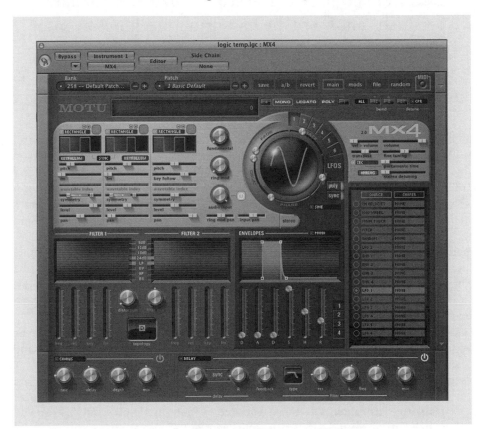

MOTU's MX4 is used here to re-create the synth ostinato from a rainy tune by a band named after the villain in a Jane Fonda sci-fi movie.

I JUST WANNA BANG ON THE LINNDRUM ALL DAY

Processing the LinnDrum to Perfection

Let's discuss my favorite drum machines of all time, the Linn LM-1 and LinnDrum (LM-2). These were originally released in 1979 and 1982, respectively, and were the first drum machines ever to exclusively utilize sampled drum sounds. We're going to discuss who used the Linn, and how you can use its killer eight-bit sounds.

The Linn was the de facto high-end drum machine for big '80s stars. Probably the most famous of them all was Prince, who used the LM-1 almost exclusively on *1999* and *Purple Rain*. That "crrrruk crrrruk" sound on "Let's Go Crazy"? That's the LM-1 sidestick sample, tuned down with the front-panel tuning knob.

Other albums making great use of the Linn include Peter Gabriel's *Security* and *Peter Gabriel* (aka "melting face"), Ultravox's *Quartet*, The Human League's *Dare*, and Don Henley's *Building the Perfect Beast*. You can also hear Linn toms pounding away in my own work with the band Berlin on the track "Scream" from the release *4Play*.

The Linn certainly sounded fat, but if you've used one, you might initially be disappointed with its dry, almost muffled sounds. The reason it doesn't sound like the records that made it famous is that its samples are bone dry. They won't have the compression, additional EQ, or "room" reverb sound that our ears have become accustomed to hearing on records. This month I'd like to go over some tricks to help create some mighty-sounding LinnDrum action!

We'll assume you'll use a virtual sampler to play back Linn samples. This works out great because the original units didn't have too much control over the samples other than volume, panning, and pitch, and we can easily re-create these with a virtual sample player.

One source for Linn samples is http://machines.hyperreal.org/manufacturers/Linn/. This will give you all the basic sounds of the LinnDrum LM-2. You can also obtain the sounds of the LM-1 in Zero-G's Nostalgia (www.soundsonline.com), a Native Instruments Kompakt-powered virtual sample-playback instrument. One approach for getting great electronic drum sounds is to split them out across a mixer as if they were a miked-up drum kit by assigning the kick, snare, hats, toms, etc. to separate mixer channels. If you're using a virtual sample player with really low system overhead (such as Logic's EXS24), you can just go the brute-force route and open a separate instance for each instrument, i.e., one sampler for kick, one for snare, etc. You can create just one keymap/program with all the drums assigned across the keyboard and then use the same instrument (i.e., keymap) for each instrument. The alternate (and more common) approach is to use one virtual instrument and assign each instrument/keymap to a separate out in order to get each drum on its own mixer channel. The degree of difficulty depends on the sequencer you're using. Personally I find this method a little tedious in Logic Pro, because each individual instrument sends its out to mixer aux object instead of emanating straight from a standard mixer channel strip. Once the individual outputs are configured, you'll want to go nuts individually processing each lovely Linn sample. Here are some tips:

• **Kick drum:** Hit this guy with a compressor for a more pronounced attack. A ratio of around 3:1 and between –6 to –10 dB of reduction works well, but the most important thing is to keep the attack control at a time over 16 ms to prevent the initial attack from getting squashed. Add a low-shelf EQ to boost around 100 Hz, and take a few dB down around 600 Hz to alleviate boxiness.
• **Snare:** Compression works well here too, but keep the attack at 20 ms or more if you want to maintain some snap in the attack. For a more '80s "blast of white noise" snare, keep the attack time low. You can use a high-shelf EQ to get more high end, and definitely send it out to a stereo reverb on an aux bus, set at between one and two seconds of decay to add a little (or a lot!) of space.
• **Cymbals:** EQ some of the low-end junk out of these so they don't interfere with other mix elements. A high-pass filter set at around 150 Hz works well. I usually "bleed" a little of the cymbals into the snare reverb, which makes for a more realistic mike-bleed effect.
• **Toms:** Compression again, with attack set in the 20 ms range to let the stick hit pop through. Dependent on tuning, you can listen for a strong fundamental resonant frequency in the toms by sweeping the frequency knob in the 150–250 Hz area, then emphasizing it with EQ. Send a bit of toms through the reverb as well.
• **Claps:** Compress and reverb the daylights out of these, and add some additional high-end brightness.

Now make sure you've panned everything as if you were looking straight at a real drum kit. Kick and snare center, hats to the right a bit, toms across the stereo field, high to low from right to left.

Now you've got rockin' LinnDrums. One more thing: Fire your drummer immediately!

SUPER (UN)NATURAL SYNTHS

Goldfrapp's "Number 1" Plasticky Strings

In the Dark Ages of electronic music, the words "synthesized strings" conjured images of just one sound the Solina String Ensemble and its closely related cousin, the ARP String Ensemble. They did one thing well: cranking out swirly approximations of a string section. In the late '70s and early '80s, fully programmable polysynths such as Sequential Circuits' Prophet-5 and Roland's Jupiter-8 made dedicated string synths redundant. As programmable polysynths became more affordable, dedicated string synths from ARP, Crumar, and Korg were almost completely tossed by the wayside.

But squished somewhere between the era of non-programmable mono synths and the revolutionary programmable polysynths were a number of "in-between" instruments such as the Moog Opus 3, ARP Quadra, and Roland Paraphonic 505. These weren't truly programmable, but they included separate—and polyphonic—brass and strings alongside a "lead synth" section. The sum of the parts wasn't truly a threat to fully programmable polysynths, but these faux polys were a little easier on the wallet than a $5,000 Prophet or Jupiter-8.

Most of these "in-between" synth ensembles have fallen between the cracks of synth history. But as long as there are vintage synth freaks out there, someone will snatch them from eBay on the cheap (or not so cheap) and put their sonically unique tones back to into action, as Will Alexander of Goldfrapp did on their chart-busting track "Number 1."

The strings in the intro and throughout the track were created using a Roland Paraphonic 505, a surprisingly flexible and warm-sounding instrument. The patch is imbued with a deep chorusing courtesy of the Paraphonic's built-in "ensemble" effect (Roland's analog stereo chorus/ensemble effect was incorporated into numerous instruments and standalone effects in the '80s and is a knockout!). An especially clever feature of the Paraphonic 505 was an input that allowed users to process external instruments. Cool, huh?

Here we'll examine how to replicate this string sound on a virtual analog synth. I used Logic Pro's ES2 plug-in, but you could use just about any full featured virtual analog synth. Starting at the basic oscillator level, we'll want to use a sawtooth wave. Since most of these "ensemble" synths were made on a budget, it's safe to stick with just one oscillator. We'll add a little LFO vibrato by assigning a triangle wave to modulate pitch. It should be very subtle, but at a fast speed (I went with 5.9 kHz). More thickness and motion will come from the chorusing and doubling we'll soon add.

Next comes the filter. This is really important to our tone, and you may need to experiment a bit to get it right. On Logic's ES2 synth, I used the band-pass filter, which should be the right choice for obtaining the characteristic "nasal" string synth tone. You may want to try high-pass filters as well, and either way, play with the cutoff and resonance controls. You'll want the filter envelope zeroed out, as this is a constant kind of tonality. You might want to have a bit of keyboard tracking dialed in order to brighten the tone as you ascend the keyboard.

Things are still pretty boring, but hang on! You might want to wait to do those fine filter tweaks until we sort out the chorusing situation, which gets us way closer to our desired tone.

Let's not forget the amplitude envelope. Here we want a simple "sustain all the way up" envelope with a medium-fast attack (about 40 ms), and a similar release time.

Now we need to replicate that great chorus sound. You can experiment with various chorus/ensemble plug-ins if you like. Not only did I use the built-in chorus effect in ES2, I "cheated" and used the unison mode, which doubles up and detunes the oscillators. This got me pretty close. But if you have a big enough chorus effect, you might not need to.

Enjoy the fakey string swirls, and think of how much money and hassle you saved by not buying and shipping one of those faux polysynth monsters from an eBay seller!

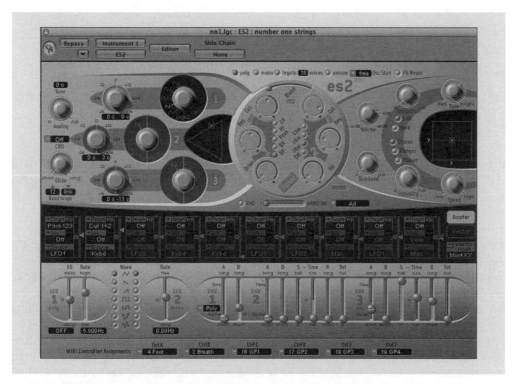

Here's what the sound of the month looks like on Logic Pro's ES2 soft synth. But just about any decent analog modeling synth, hardware or software, can create this patch.

ONE HAND CLAPPING

Creating the Handclap Smash

When I was just a wee tot of a synth geek, MTV kindly delivered British synth music to my living room. One of the artists MTV opened my eyes to was the seminal synth band Yaz, featuring the talents of Depeche Mode's then recently departed keyboardist Vince Clarke. Clarke was already a programming whiz back then, and he made great use of the Roland TR-808, particularly with the prominent handclap "smash" featured in the monster club tracks "Don't Go" and "Situation." As a slightly older synth geek, I sampled the clap from "Situation" and used it in a whole bunch of awful four-track demos. But making 'em yourself is more fun!

The clap in "Situation" is a standard Roland TR- 808 clap with a some added compression and a bunch of reverb. But we can roll our own version using a soft synth and have more flexibility, specifically in getting the extra decay for full "smash," as opposed to the short clap of the original Roland TR-808 and TR-909 drum machines.

Let's analyze the anatomy of a clap. First of all, we need to establish a basic sound generator, i.e., the oscillator. Since a clap doesn't really have a discernible pitch, we can use a white noise generator. On its own, white noise is anything but percusssive. For all intents and purposes, it's a nonstop wall of, well, noise containing an equal amount of all frequencies occurring simultaneously. We could just throw an envelope generator on it to give it the basic snappy attack characteristic of a percussion sound, but this won't sound anything like a clap. There are two specific things we can do to transform our plain vanilla noise into glorious clap smashdom.

First, we can filter and EQ our white noise like crazy! You'll want to use a standard low-pass filter, modulated by an envelope generator with instant attack, and about 300 ms of decay and release. Set the filter cutoff and envelope modulation level so that the filter is almost all the way open on attack and then fades to about 30 percent open. If you can run it through a high-pass filter to knock off most of the lows as well, that's great; otherwise, you can use EQ (more on this later).

The amplitude envelope will be very similar to the one I just described above. Just make sure to have the sustain all way down: Otherwise, our little clapping gnomes will get their hands stuck together! Now that we've got some nicely enveloped noise, we want use some EQ to further mangle it. If you didn't already, use a high-pass filter (or low shelving) to knock out all the lows below 150 Hz. Then we'll add a couple of strong mid-frequency peaks. Add about 8 dB at 440 Hz for body, and around 14 dB at 1,200 Hz for snap. You may need to experiment a little with the EQ, but don't be subtle with these, they make all the difference between simple noise and clap-smack-o-rama.

At this point, you'll have something that doesn't sound exactly like a clap, but it's a wicked "smack" noise. The attack portion doesn't sound that clap-like, but if you're layering it with a snare drum, that might not be too important. You'll certainly want to throw a nice, big reverb on it (and make it obnoxiously loud in the mix). This may be all you need for drum-smash nirvana, but if you really want your claps to be as clappy as can be, read on.

To replicate the irregular attack portion of a bunch of little hands smacking together inside a Roland drum machine, use of the following methods to briefly dirty up the attack of the sound. You can use an LFO set to a sawtooth wave to modulate the filter cutoff frequency very quickly, or the VCA volume. The end result is pretty similar. The tricky part is that the LFO has to be cycling pretty fast; around 50 Hz is optimal, and many synths' LFOs won't run that quickly. The other hard part is that you only want this modulation for the first 100 ms or so, then you want the LFO effect to go away. If the soft synth you're using has a LFO fade-in parameter with a negative setting, this works great. In other words, you want to set it so that the LFO starts out on, then quickly turns off after about 100 ms. MOTU's MX4 synth and Logic's ES2 both have this parameter. Logic's Ultrabeat has a very useful LFO parameter that lets you set exactly how many cycles it stays on for before it shuts off; it's designed specifically for this task.

Have fun with theses synthesized claps, and try mixing it up with EQ and envelope settings for new sounds!

Here is the basic clap smash, sans tricky attack portion modulation, using GMedia Oddity.

LET ME BLOW YA MIND

No, Not with Drugs—with Analog Polysynth Brass!

I admit that I'm completely obsessed with the whirling, swirling tonalities of plasticky fake string tones. But all strings and no brass make Mitch a dull . . . I dunno what, so in the interest of widening our tonal palette, let's swing over to the other side of the analog orchestra pit to reflect on the blatting, blasting world of artificial analog brass sounds.

Everyone knows that brass instruments can only produce one note at a time. Naturally, brass sections comprised of multiple players are used to create chords and multi-part, moving musical phrases. In the analog synthesizer world, early instruments could only play one note at a time, just like their acoustic counterparts, so re-creating solo brass instruments was relatively easy, but brass sections were a lot tougher. Unless you had a whole lotta Moog, or your name was Wendy Carlos, you were out of luck. Luckily the arrival of polyphonic synthesizers in the late '70s and early '80s changed all this. Because of their polyphonic nature, that is, the ability to play multiple notes at once, players could easily create the kind of clustered, two-fisted chord density of a real brass section.

Initially crude "ensemble" preset synths like the ARP Omni and Moog Opus 3 made acceptable synth brass sounds, but the arrival of the heavyweight programmable polyphonic analog synthesizers really set the tone for the powerful, honking, analog synth brass as we know it today. These include the Roland Jupiter-8, Sequential Circuits Prophet-5, and Oberheim OB series synths, among others.

Generally speaking, big sawtooth waves make for great brass tones. They work great because bright, loudly played brass instruments such as trumpet and saxophone contain lots of even-order harmonics, and sawtooth waveforms are very similar in nature. Since we're trying to replicate a big, juicy brass section, we want to break out all the horsepower we've got. If you have a two-oscillator synth, use both, and detune one slightly from the other. You'll want to stop just short of things sounding ugly, but don't be shy; real brass ensembles are slightly less than perfect. If you have a third oscillator available, use it, and detune it in the opposite direction of the second oscillator. You can also tune up or down an octave to make things bigger, though I prefer to just play the octaves and keep on overdubbing more parts for "bigness."

Brass instruments involve an actual person blowing into them (see how educational this book is?), and we'll use the filter to replicate this effect. Begin with the filter cutoff closed down most of the way. Use the envelope amount control to apply the filter's dedicated envelope generator to the cutoff frequency. We want to end up with a bright sound, but we've closed down the initial filter cutoff setting because the envelope generator adds to the initial setting. Now we'll set the filter envelope attack to around 60 ms. Pretty quick, but not instant. Crank the sustain all the way up so we can hold our note consistently. You want to hear the filter open up quick then stay almost all the way open. Turn the resonance up a bit to make our brass a little more realistic and less "synth waveform" perfect. Stop short of it sounding like a wah-ing Moog!

Your amplitude envelope settings should be similar to the filter settings, though you can make the attack faster, since the filter opening will take care of the volume rise anyway. Again, sustain will be full up, and release should be pretty quick; horns stop making noise real quick when you stop blowing into them (again with the education . . .).

Effects are really your friends here. Chorusing will give the illusion of more horns playing, which is what we really want. Use just enough so it doesn't sound artificial. And a nice, warm reverb will make things far more realistic. Now go and toot your own horns!

Native Instruments Reaktor 5 is capable of incredibly wild sonic mayhem, but it's also just the thing for experimenting with basic synthesis. You can call up a nice two-oscillator preset and get your synth brass sounds dialed up in no time.

SYNTH BASS LAYERS

Build Better Bass Through Technology

Along, long time ago, in a galaxy far, far away—well, actually, in Detroit—I read an interview in these very pages with a young Thomas Dolby, then riding high on the success of his hit, "She Blinded Me with Science." In it, he mentioned that the Moog Micromoog was his favorite bass synth, and talked about how the standard, fuzzy, three-oscillator chorused Minimoog bass was just sometimes too much for him. The Micromoog, on the other hand, was a budget synth—just one oscillator, it had very limited tonal resources. Thomas's words must have stuck with me, as I've been partial to single-oscillator bass sounds ever since. They sit very nicely in the mix and provide only a foundation to build upon, just like a bass guitar, which also has "one oscillator" per note: the string.

Single-oscillator basses are great for "bassic" purposes, but what if you really want things to sound large? You could just make a bigger, beefier bass sound. That works, but the low end of the spectrum can get a little smeared and furry. Instead I like to keep my solid one-oscillator bass sound and combine it with another bass sound created specifically for high-end bass duties. Simply make a new instrument track in your sequencer, copy the MIDI data, and use a separate soft synth to make the second sound. The combination makes for a stellar one-two punch, and since they're separate instruments, you can really optimize the "bass" and "treble" tones.

Let's get it started. First, we want to create our foundation sound. I usually create something approximating a bass guitar played with a pick (the Thompson Twins' "Hold Me Now" track is a perfect example). Start with a low-tuned oscillator set to a sawtooth wave. The filter cutoff frequency should be almost all the way down. Instead of opening the cutoff manually, we'll use the filter envelope to control the cutoff frequency. Turn the filter envelope mod full up, and set the filter envelope controls with the attack on zero and the decay medium—just like a bass guitar string decaying. Sustain can be relatively low, and release pretty quick. You can set the amplitude envelope to a basic on/off shape, with a quick attack, full sustain, and a quick release.

Now that we have our basic sound, we can make a high-end sound. There are a lot of options here, but I'm going to detail what I did in one of my own tracks, "New York Girls," from my CD *Nightlife* by Celebutante (plug alert!). Using the ES2 soft synth in Logic Pro, I augmented the foundation bass with a sonically complex stereo chorused and distorted tone. This is a three-oscillator patch, with all the wave-forms set on sawtooth waves. The tricky part is that oscillator two is tuned up a fifth from oscillator one, and oscillator three is tuned down two octaves from oscillator one (oscillator three's volume should be somewhat quiet compared to one and two). Note that the distortion effect we will soon apply tends to mask the built-in fifth interval.

I used a lot of filter resonance, and slowly manipulated the cutoff frequency throughout the verses. The actual cutoff setting should be really dull, because the heavy distortion effect will radically alter its character. The amplitude envelope should be of the on/off variety.

Now add a heavy distortion plug-in after the synth, followed by an EQ. The sound will be way thick, so we'll use a low-shelf EQ to seriously reduce frequencies below 300 Hz; set it to –18 dB. This will get rid of excess low-end mud. I also put a –6 dB dip in at 1,600 Hz to reduce harshness. You may need to experiment a little with these settings, but remember that all low-end fatness (around 150 Hz and down) is handled by the other bass sound.

Finally, I used Logic's "Spreader" plug-in, which is a sort of chorus, but any chorus/doubler plug would work great for extra "stereoizing." Though this sound is harmonically rich and spatially wide, it isn't intended to contain much low-end girth.

You can download audio examples and the Logic ES2 synth patches of these sounds at www.celebu-tantemusic.com/keybmag and at keyboardmag.com. Happy layering!

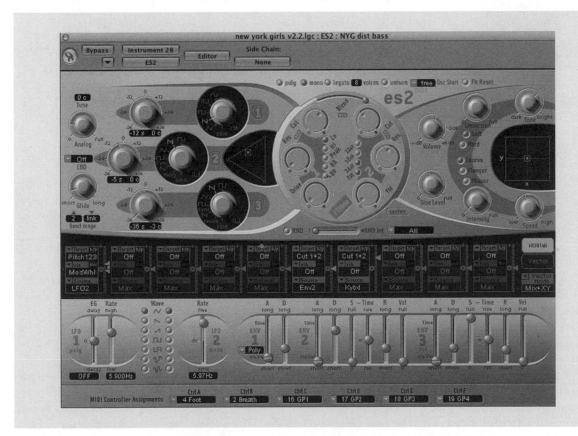

Using the ES2 soft synth in Apple Logic, I created this three-oscillator distorted bass sound. But this is just for the high-end beef that I layered with my simple single-oscillator patch. Layering bass sounds is a great way to get a fatter sound without muddying up your mix.

IF YOU HEAR A SOLO, TAKE IT

Steve Winwood's Famous Lead Synth Sound

ignature. Ponder the word for a moment. How many of us wish we had a sound or style that was instantly recognizable by millions? Whether deliberate or just a happy accident, a truly defining sound is one of the hallmarks of the greats. Steve Winwood has had plenty of amazing career achievements. One the coolest ones is his trademarked rubbery synth lead sound. This sound owes as much to programming as it does playing technique, and we'll cover both.

Probably the most famous Winwood track to feature it is "If You See a Chance" from his 1980 release, *Arc of a Diver.* Steve must have known he was on to something because it's featured on two other *Arc* tracks, "Second Hand Woman," and "Slowdown Sundown." The Winwood lead sound would continue to show up throughout his career on tracks such as "The Finer Things" and "Valerie."

The original "If You See a Chance" lead emanated from a Sequential Circuits Prophet-5 or Prophet-10. These are functionally identical; basically a Prophet-10 is two Prophet-5s in one box. You can see Steve rocking a very rare Prophet-10 in the super-hip '80s video for "If You See a Chance." In fact, the *Arc of a Diver"* disc may as well be a full-blown demonstration record for the Prophet synths! On his later releases, Steve become a Yamaha endorser, and the DX7 FM synthesis sound is all over *Back in the High Life.* I suspect his signature lead sound became an FM approximation at this point, as it doesn't seem to have the analog grit and "spittiness" it did on *Arc of a Diver.* Try listening on really nice near-fields or headphones, it sounds great!

So let's talk about how we can make this bad boy, huh? If you have a virtual synth that approximates a Prophet-5, that's the best choice. The most common one is Native Instruments' Pro-53, but you could also use Arturia's new Prophet V, or maybe you're one of those lucky devils with a new Creamware Pro-12 ASB hardware synth module. Don't be discouraged if you don't have any of these. You can get pretty close with many common two-oscillator virtual synths.

We'll use two oscillators to start, both set to pulse waveforms. Using the pulse-width control, set the width, aka "duty cycle," to a very narrow setting. We don't want the width so narrow that the sound completely cuts out, but about 20 percent is good (you can compare it with the "rawwave" file I have posted on my website at the end of this piece). You'll want the oscillators tuned almost exactly the same. It is *really* important to nail this sound. If you're using a Pro-53, set the "fine" tune on osc B all the way down, but make sure the "analog" knob is up around ten o' clock for the slightest amount of very slow beating; you can compare to my "heldnote" file online to get the idea.

You'll want to use a low-pass filter with the cutoff frequency about 80 percent open. Dial in a little resonance, say about 20 percent. The amplitude envelope is a simple on/off, i.e., instant attack and decay, full sustain, and instant release. Be sure to set your pitch and mod wheels too: A whole-step pitch-bend range and some medium speed vibrato on the mod wheel is what we're looking for.

I also recommend a little EQ and reverb on the audio mixer channel. I used a Waves Renaissance EQ low-shelf EQ set at –9 dB with a corner frequency of 351 Hz. You'll find that hacking out low end like this makes sounds have a little less impact, but it'll sit better in a mix and sound much more like a recording. Listen to "If You See a Chance" and you'll see what I mean.

And now for the other part. "What other part?" I hear you say. (I hear voices sometimes. That's normal, right?) The other part is Mr. Winwood's virtuosic use of the pitch and mod wheels. Virtually all of the tracks using this sound make great use of smooth full-step bends and tastefully applied vibrato. You may need to, uh, what's that word for that thing I never do? Oh yeah, *practice* to get that down. Smoothness and knowing where you're going and need to end up are the secret here. Have fun, and be sure to check out www.celebutantemusic.com/keybmag for audio examples and the Pro-53 patch.

Wail like Winwood, virtually. Native Instruments' Pro-53 can help you imitate his trademark Prophet-5 tone.

STRING ENCOUNTERS
OF THE SECOND KIND

Spooky Strings, Polymoog Style

This month's installment of "Vintage Sounds" could be considered part two of my first column, way back in the Feb. '05 issue, wherein I discussed how to coax dark, swirling string textures reminiscent of the classic Prophet-5 synthesizer. Here we'll explore a different but equally evocative flavor of faux-string darkdom, something I like to call "The Gary Numan Spooky Polymoog Strings!"—also known as the "Vox Humana" factory preset of the Polymoog 280A keyboard.

Though Gary Numan enjoys great success in England, most Stateside dwellers know him only from his trademark track, "Cars," from his album *The Pleasure Principle*, which featured the Moog Polymoog and its uniquely seasick string sound on almost every track. You can also hear Polymoog strings on Blondie's megahit "Heart of Glass." The discos were awash in Polymoog string swirls circa 1979!

Creating this sound is relatively straightforward, with a few tricks to getting it just right. You can get pretty close on most virtual polysynths, so fire one up and let's go!

Starting at the oscillator level, set oscillator one and two to sawtooth waves, and tune them to the same octave and pitch. You can detune them a little bit; just enough for a mild chorusing effect. Here's the most important thing about nailing the sound: Set an LFO to a triangle wave and apply vibrato to only *one* of the oscillators. We want a slow vibrato with slightly more depth than you would usually use. Oscillator two should have a seasick quality to it. If your synth displays the LFO speed, I've found around 3.8 Hz to be optimum. You'll notice that the vibrato-free oscillator one has the effect of "gluing" the sound together so that we can get away with an almost hideous degree of vibrato on oscillator two.

If you really want authenticity, then stick with just the two oscillators. You can beef things up using stacked unison/poly modes. But be careful not to stack voices to the point where notes get cut off. We'll explain this a little later, but let's talk about filters for a moment.

If you listen to some of the Numan tracks on *The Pleasure Principle* album, you can clearly hear that the filters are not of the standard low-pass variety, but instead have a middy, resonant, almost vocal quality to them. This was a result of the Polymoog keyboard's unique "resonators," which amounted to 6 dB per octave fixed-frequency inductor-based filters (say that five times fast). The Polymoog also had one master voltage-controlled filter for all its oscillators, so instead of controlling cutoff with an envelope, you'll want to make a fixed setting (i.e., no filter envelopes applied) and leave it. I've found the Nord Lead's band-pass and high-pass modes to be pretty good at emulating this sound, and most soft synths these days have similar filter options. The best way to dial these in is to experiment with cutoff and mid to high resonance settings until things start to take on a vocal quality. Don't let it get too bright; we're trying to set a mood here.

As for amplitude envelopes, we'll need a slow attack, infinite sustain so you can hold down notes forever, and a *loooong* release time in the vicinity of 2–5 seconds(!). When playing melody lines, notes will have a smearing effect as they fade away (as well as letting everyone know just what a distraught android you truly are). This is why we don't want to stack up too many oscillators. If you do, the synth may well run out of polyphony and start stealing notes, thereby eradicating all of the beautiful note releases. The Polymoog was well suited to this effect, as its unusual voice architecture gave it unlimited polyphony.

Finally, a slow delay effect (400–800 ms, depending on song tempo) is usually effective, and gives the auditory illusion of more beating, chorusing oscillators stacked upon each other. I find actual chorusing effects should be avoided as the characteristic sound takes off some of the creepy edge. Phasers, on the other hand are great—"Cars" made use of MXR's popular Phase 100 stomp box.

You can hear a short demo of this sound created with a Roland Jupiter-8 synth at www.keyboardmag. com and www.celebutantemusic.com/keybmag. Now go put on that spacesuit and crank up that swirling string siren song!

The real ARP 2600 was strictly monophonic, but Arturia's virtual ARP 2600 V adds polyphony, which makes it an awesome spooky string synth. Here we use VCO3 as an LFO to add vibrato mod to VCO2.

ADDENDUM

Since writing this piece back in 2006, I've done more research on the classic Moog Polymoog Keyboard's "Vox Humana" patch, aka the Gary Numan patch. It's a popular topic on forums, and I've never heard it nailed just right in the virtual synth world. My article on re-creating it was pretty close, but recently I stumbled upon some information about the Polymoog synthesizer's voice architecture that illuminated how to *very accurately* re-create the "Vox Humana" patch.

The Polymoog is a rather elaborate top-octave divide system (TOS) instrument. Prior to microprocessor-powered voice-assign synths that sense key presses and assign notes to a handful of oscillators (such as the Prophet-5, Oberheim OB-series, etc.), organs, string machines, and synths used 12 square-wave oscillators representing each note of the scale at a high pitch. The oscillators' frequencies were halved repeatedly to cover the entire range of the keyboard. This has the advantage of giving an instrument full polyphony, i.e., all keys can be pressed simultaneously. But it imposes severe limitations upon individual note filter and amplitude articulation, because once a note is struck, all other notes will pick up wherever the first note was in a filter or volume envelope.

The Polymoog contained two independent TOS oscillator circuits to allow detuning and different waveforms for each. Since the octave division chips of a TOS system inherently output square waves only, Moog developed a custom chip with circuits to convert the square waves to a ramp wave for one of the oscillators, and a variable pulse wave for the other. The "Polycom" chip, as it was called, cost Moog a fortune, and the Polymoog used one of these chips under each of its 71 keys. No wonder the Polymoog cost five grand!

Many people in online forums will argue that the unique "Vox Humana" patch is a result of the Polymoog keyboard's unusual fixed inductor-based filters (i.e., coils), but I beg to differ. For all its odd limitations, the Polymoog has one feature I don't think I've ever seen in a vintage analog polysynth—three independent low-frequency modulation oscillators. The routings are fixed with two hard-wired to each oscillator bank's frequency, and one modulating the width of the pulse wave. As you may know, pulse-width modulation has a very unique tone, but typically isn't used in conjunction with pitch mod (i.e., vibrato). This is because most vintage analog synths usually only have one LFO, and the best-sounding rate for PWM isn't necessarily best for vibrato (not to mention hearing PWM and pitch moving at the exact same rate doesn't make for interesting sound animation). But the Polymoog could easily modulate each oscillator bank's pitch at independent speeds—*while modulating the PWM of one of the oscillators at a different speed and depth*—which gives a very unique timbral and vibrato warble. Here lies the elusive secret that is "Vox Humana"!

If we're going to re-create "Vox Humana" on a virtual analog instrument, we'll need one with three separate LFO's. I had excellent results with Arturia Jupiter-8V; not only does it have the "standard" Jupiter LFO on its front panel, it contains two extra LFOs hidden within its mod tab under the "Galaxy" section. You can use just about any virtual analog, but it *must* have three LFOs. Let's get to it!

Choose a saw wave for oscillator one, and a variable pulse wave for oscillator two. Set their octave controls the same (8' in this case), and set their volumes equally in the oscillator mixer section.

Moving on to the filter, I set the Jupiter to 12 dB/oct mode for a little more mid-buzz, and set the frequency to 678 Hz (medium) and the filter mod control to 0.375. Resonance is at zero. Env 1 (filter env) attack is at 378 ms, decay at zero, sustain full up, and release a slow 8300 ms. Amplitude envelope should be set identically, though you can dial in attack and release to taste.

Now for the modulation trickery . . . first, we'll apply pulse-width mod to oscillator two's pulse wave. In the LFO section, set the rate at about 4.5 Hz, and select a sine wave. Moving over to the VCO modulator, set the PWM slider at 0.5, and the three-way switch to LFO. Now we'll add vibrato to the oscillators. Click the "Open" button at the top right, then click "Galaxy" at the left. Set both LFOs to triangle waves. Set LFO one's rate to 3.5 Hz and LFO two's rate to 5.0 Hz. The exact rates of all three LFOs aren't critical, just make sure they're all different. Now set the routing to the oscillators' pitch in the Y and X output windows to the right. Choose "VCO1 Pitch" from the first pop-up menu in the Y output box and set the depth knob at 0.072. Now choose "VCO2 Pitch" from the first pop-up menu in the X output box and set its depth knob at 0.052. Again, exact settings aren't crucial here, just mix 'em up a bit.

That's it! A perfect, uh, "replica" of "Vox Humana" (boo, hiss!).

Here you can see how I've used the Jupiter 8V's extra LFOs in its "Galaxy" mod section. Galaxy mod allows unique mixing of two mod sources, but here we're just using the LFOs independently.

Oscillator Hard
Sync Secrets

'd be willing to bet that the lead synth riff that kicks off the Cars' "Let's Go" is one of the most recognizable pieces of electronic music ever devised. And it's probably safe to say that this riff inspired many to play something other than electric guitar! After enduring many years of listening to people muck it up (along with Harold Faltemeyer's cool hook on "Axel F"), I'm here to help y'all nail Greg Hawkes's vintage 1979 synth wizardry.

"Let's Go" makes use of oscillator hard sync, a way of locking up two analog oscillators to create unique high-end harmonics. You can also hear the "Let's Go" sound reprised almost exactly on No Doubt's megahit "Just a Girl" in an affectionate tip of the hat. Oscillator sync is also used in a more subtle way on Kraftwerk's "Neon Lights" (mainly a result of tasteful application of a low-pass filter). And next time you're watching the classic Chevy Chase comedy *Fletch*, listen to the cool '80s sound track; its sound track is chock-full of synced-oscillator goodness. And check out Dave Diamond's classic sync solo on Berlin's '80's chestnut "The Metro."

At the end of the '70s, Greg Hawkes made excellent use of the then-brand-new Sequential Circuits Prophet-5. Most folks were pretty excited about the Prophet's five-voice polyphony and easy digital patch storage, but oscillator sync and cross modulation were pretty sweet features back then too. ARP synths often had sync capabilities, but most compact Moogs lacked it.

Lucky for us, sync is included in many stand-alone and plug-in virtual analog synths, so replicating the sound is pretty easy. Here's how it works: oscillator sync is an analog synth trick where a "slave" oscillator is forced to restart its waveform cycle every time the master oscillator begins its cycle. The master oscillator's controls function as usual, but the slave oscillator behaves a little differently. Instead of controlling pitch in the standard fashion, the slave oscillator's pitch controls act like more of a harmonic color control. The higher the tuning, the more crazy high-order harmonics occur. These high harmonics normally stay in constant relationship to the master oscillator. But things start sounding wild if you quickly sweep the pitch of the slave oscillator. Of course, it's not practical to twist the pitch knob of the slave oscillator like crazy, so instead we can use an envelope generator or a low-frequency oscillator to do the knob twisting for us. This is the basic concept of voltage-controlled synthesis—letting a constantly changing voltage automate the knob twisting. In the case of virtual analog synths, there's no actual voltage, only a digital re-creation inside a computer, but the concept is the same. Here I used Native Instruments' Pro-53, but Aruturia's Pro-V works great as well.

Begin by setting two oscillators to square waves. Sync will work with any waveform, but it is most frequently applied to square and sawtooths, as its brash tonality is well suited to harmonically rich waveforms. One of the oscillators should have a "sync" button; turn that baby on! Now we need to get our pitch sweep going. If your synth has a pitch envelope, route it to oscillator one, but not oscillator two (depending on the synth, it may be the other way around). If you're using a Native Instruments Pro-53 like I did, use the "POLY-MOD" section to route the filter envelope to control oscillator one's pitch by turning the "FILT ENV" knob up about three-quarters and selecting the "FREQ A" destination button. Now set the filter envelope for medium-quick attack and release. It may take a little time to get the "FILT ENV" and oscillator one frequency knobs tweaked just right, but all the variations are half the fun! Turn up oscillator one in the mixer controls; we only need to hear the synced oscillator.

Set the filter wide open with no envelope control and zero resonance. The amplitude envelope should be set to "on/off," i.e., zero attack and decay, full sustain, and quick release. Finally, if your synth has a "unison" mode, try that, as synced and stacked oscillators are made for each other!

You can download some audio samples, as well as a Native Instruments Pro-53 patch, at www.celebutantemusic.com/keybmag and www.keyboardmag.com.

A Native Instruments Pro-53 can be used to sync oscillators and get the classic "Let's Go" sound.

DELAYED REACTION

Classic Synth Delay Techniques from Yaz

Tired of mundane synth riffs? With a delay effect, it's easy to turn a boring bass line or a lousy lead into the best hook ever. A delay simply takes the incoming audio and repeats it a little later, by a set duration, then mixes it with the dry incoming signal. When the delay time is in sync with the tempo and rhythm of the song, a new world of hypnotic echoing effects opens up.

One of the classic '80s dance-floor anthems is Yaz's "Situation." Blending English New Wave with early Detroit techno, the opening riff is an instantly recognizable minor-key delay motif. Surely every Midwest kid has heard the Steve Miller Band's spooky intro to "Fly Like an Eagle," created with simple square waves and white-keys-only glisses. Duran Duran's "Save a Prayer" took a simple eighth-note minor motif and made it special with a triplet delay. And the signature riff of Howard Jones's "New Song" made use of an unusually long whole-note delay for a unique call-and-response "round" effect.

Back to Yaz . . . for the main riff in "Situation," Vince Clarke used a Sequential Circuits Pro-One synthesizer. This was a compact, non-programmable mono analog synth containing the same voice circuits as its big brother, the Prophet-5. Clarke did some pretty awesome programming back then; he used the Pro-One almost exclusively throughout the *Upstairs At Eric's* record.

The main ingredient for the sound involves pulse-width modulation, or PWM. PWM occurs when the width of a square or pulse waveform is changed while it's playing, usually by an LFO (for constant movement) or an envelope generator (for a one-shot sweep). This gives the waveform evolving harmonic content, and also changes its pitch minutely over time, lending a desirable chorusing effect.

Set the basic waves for two oscillators to a square wave in the same octave; they should both have the same settings. Detune one of the oscillators by about 12 cents. Then set an LFO to modulate the pulse width ever so slightly; just enough for a little warble. The LFO speed should be about 3.3 Hz, and depth should be very small; I used about 0.1 percent. If your synth allows it, you can use the same LFO to modulate the pitch of the oscillators for a tiny bit of vibrato as well.

Next, set a low-pass filter to about 30 percent open. Then use your synth's filter envelope to modulate the cutoff. I used a quick attack, 570 ms of decay, zero sustain, and 100 ms release. This quickly moves our filter settings. Set the amplitude envelope the same as the filter, but add some sustain so we can hear the held notes a bit.

Now we're in the ballpark. As I tweaked, I found I could duplicate the, um, situation, more accurately by adding some warm overdrive distortion before the delay. Since the riff never plays two notes simultaneously, you won't hear the nasty intermodulation between notes that usually comes with distortion effects. Overdrive often has a great effect with moving PWM sounds, so stash this in your book of tricks! I also added a big chunk of Logic ES2's built-in chorus to widen the tone. If your synth doesn't have a built-in chorus, just add some from a plug-in. Now let's play a lick:

Are you thinking what I'm thinking? We need to add a delay to make this line really great. The original tempo of "Situation" is about 118 bpm. We need an eighth-note delay, so the time would be 253 ms. Most sequencer hosts and delay plug-ins will sync automatically; just set the note value to eighth notes. For best results, add the delay on an effects send bus, and send the dry signal to it. This will simplify independent panning of wet and dry signals. If you use the delay on a bus send, make sure to set it to 100 percent wet. Now pan the dry synth to about 10 o' clock to the left, and the delay to about 2 o' clock.

For the finishing touch, cut some lows out with an EQ, and add a big, juicy reverb. You can download audio examples and the Logic ES2 patch at www.celebutantemusic/keybmag or at www.keyboardmag.com. Now don't mess around . . . move out!

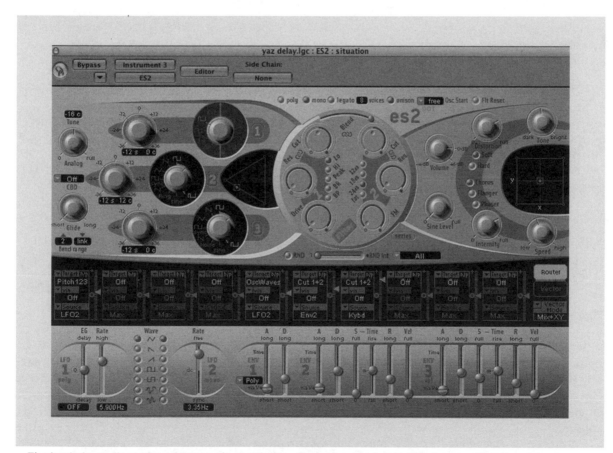

The basic ingredients for a Yaz-worthy synth line, shown here in Apple ES2: two oscillators set to square waves, detuned slightly, modulated with PWM, and delayed by an eighth-note value.

LORDS OF THE DISTORTED UNDERWORLD

Get Creative with Synth Distortion

For some reason or other, distortion has always been viewed as an effect for guitarists only. Synth guys are there to back up macho guitar players with clean pads and pianos, right? Wrong! The tide started to turn in the '70s, when Jan Hammer made a dent by sending his Minimoogs and Oberheim SEM modules through distorted Marshall amps and going head to head with the likes of Jeff Beck and John McLaughlin in the fusion world. (His keytar-swingin' rock posturing didn't hurt either.) And with the advent of techno in the '90s, someone figured out that running Roland's chintzy TB-303 bass-line synth through a distortion pedal sounded cool in an obnoxious way, and the voice of the rave was born.

Although there's a lot of faux-lead guitar and 303 patches out there, you can still explore new sonic variations with synth distortion. One of my favorites is featured prominently in the Underworld track "Rez/Cowgirl" from their *Everything, Everything* live CD and the concert video of the same name. It consists of a pretty clever use of filter resonance as an evolving tone source all its own; sort of a variation on the Roland TB-303/distortion theme. I also made use of this trick on the track "Shiny" on the Berlin release *Voyeur*.

A repeating arpeggiated motif is important for the proper effect, but first let's cook up the sound. We'll start with a two-oscillator patch, with both oscillators set to square waves. Square waves tend to work well with distortion as the extreme "on/off" nature of the waveform seems to hit distortion circuitry pretty hard. Set both oscillators to the same octave and detune one a couple of cents from the other.

The filter cutoff is going to be manipulated while you're playing, so its setting isn't important now. You'll want the resonance at least 75 percent up, or almost all the way, depending on the synth. The filter envelope should be off. The amp should be just an "on/off" type (attack zero, decay long, sustain long, release very quick).

Now let's make the arpeggiated riff. I chose something similar to the Underworld track:

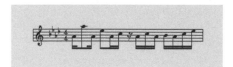

You can experiment with different riffs, but it's usually a good idea to stick with something simple, like an eighth-note sequence, as the filter motion will give the sonic illusion of many more notes playing.

Now it's time to choose your weapon. You can use a distortion plug-in from your host program, but I really strongly recommend routing it to a separate audio interface out and making use of an actual overdrive or distortion stomp box, as they usually have more personality than plug-ins. They also tend to have less icky, digital artifact overtones. For these examples, I used a Pro-Co RAT, but I've also had great results with Boss Super Overdrive pedals.

Delay sounds great here too. If you're going with external distortion, you'll probably need to use an outboard delay. You'll want to try a quarter-note or eighth-note triplet delay, with minimal feedback.

Here's where the fun begins. Once you have everything set up, you'll want to fine-tune the resonance. Make sure that the filter envelope controls are completely off, as we want the resonance to emit a single steady tone as the notes play. The basis of the sound is in the way the steady state resonance interacts with the changing arpeggiated notes. We want the resonance knob high enough that the filter tone really rings, but low enough that it doesn't drown out the arpeggiated notes emitting from the oscillators. This may take some experimentation, but you'll know when you hit the sweet spot. Once you have, open and close the filter very slowly. Listen closely as you play so that you catch the interesting areas where notes ring harmoniously. And make sure to get a lot of mileage out of closed-down filter settings where the arpeggiated notes aren't really audible, but the resonant noises precariously bounce around. Finally, try assigning the filter cutoff to cool expressive controllers. For the Berlin "Shiny" track, I disabled the pitch bend on my Roland Jupiter-6's joystick and set it to control the cutoff frequency only, which gave me really accurate control. You can download audio examples at www.celebutantemusic/keybmag or at www.keyboardmag.com. Go forth and distort everything, everything!

THE SYNTHS ARE ALRIGHT

The Secret Synth on the Who's "Won't Get Fooled Again"? An Organ.

NOVEMBER 2006

Rock star excess. In the late '60s and early '70s, blowing your hard-earned rock god cash on women, cars, and illicit substances was the name of the game. The Who certainly did their share. But while the famously party-happy Keith Moon was driving his Bentley into swimming pools, mad genius Pete Townshend was busy buying into the bleeding-edge world of analog synthesizers, putting them to use on classic Who records such as *Who's Next* and the brilliant sound track for *Tommy*. Townshend's guitar hero status looms so largely that it often obscures his achievements as one of the early synth innovators. His use of synths and processed organ on "Won't Get Fooled Again," as well as "Baba O' Riley" from *Who's Next*, are some of the most recognizable riffs in rock history.

Townshend is usually associated with the very first ARP 2500 and 2600 synths (ARP featured Pete in a series of pretty groovy print ads back in the day!). But many are unaware that "Won't Get Fooled Again" wasn't played on a synthesizer at all; it was actually a Lowrey Berkshire Deluxe TBO-1 organ processed with the filter section of an EMS Synthi VCS3. Apparently Pete hadn't quite figured out his then-new massive ARP 2500 modular synth while making the demos for *Who's Next*. Instead he made use of the somewhat simpler VCS3, an odd little beast later made famous by Pink Floyd and Brian Eno.

One interesting aspect of the "Won't Get Fooled Again" sound is that Townshend is actually just holding down sustained chords; the pulsing eighth-note rhythm is created by modulating the VCA with a square-wave LFO.

You can make a similar patch by using a virtual synth on its own, but I thought it would be more authentic if we created this sound just like Pete did by patching an organ into a filter. I used a Native Instruments B4-organ virtual instrument followed by Ohm Force's Quad Frohmage Filter multi-effect plug-in.

Let's do it!

First, we need to get our organ sound. You can use anything that outputs a pretty wide-open organ sound with most of the drawbars out, such as B4 or Logic EVB3. Since the drawbars themselves act as a set of filters, the idea is to initially achieve a harmonically rich sound to feed into the sweeping filter, giving it something to work with. If the organ is too dull, the sweeping filter will just make it duller. The drawbar setting I used was as follows: 888888333 (see illustration). As long as it's pretty open, the drawbar settings aren't too critical. Be sure to shut off all percussion, vibrato, rotary speaker, and distortion effects! We want a totally clean organ tone.

The filter is where things get a little tricky. Keep in mind that you can use just about any resonating low-pass filter that allows LFO modulation. I used Quad Frohmage because it contains multiple filters that can be set in series mode, i.e., one after the other. If you press the "1/2" button in the "probe and routing" window at the top, the first two modules ("bands" in Frohm-speak) will be put in series. The first filter handles the slow open-and-close filter sweep. This is a low-pass filter with a little resonance, with the cutoff frequency swept by an LFO set to approximately 0.275 Hz (Frohmage shows this as "2.75 per second"). You may have to tweak the cutoff and depth a little to get it right.

We have two options for the eighth-note pulsing effect. You use the sound as described above and simply play eighth-note chords. But if you have Frohmage or another filter that offers two filters in series, you can set up the second filter to pulse the sound. Use a square wave LFO to modulate the cutoff frequency from all the way closed to wide open at around 4.25 Hz (0.2100 per sec in Frohm-speak). You can

also use a synth's amp section to accomplish the same thing, but stand-alone filters are more common.

Now throw a little virtual spring reverb on our patch and start swinging that mike around like mad! (Watch out for small pets, please.) YEAAAAAAAAAHH-HHHHHHHH!!!!!

Ohm Force's Quad Frohmage filter plug-in processes the basic organ tone to get that nasty "Won't Get Fooled Again" sound.

The basic ingredient of this famous sound is right here: Turn off all rotary simulation, percussion, chorus, and other effects, and pull your organ's drawbar's first six drawbars out to 8, and the last three out to 3.

808 Kicks to Knock Down the Walls

BOOM. BOOM-BOOM, BOOM. It's hard to fathom that some pocket-protector-wearing propeller-head engineers accidentally created the ubiquitous Roland TR-808 boom kick that's blown countless woofers, but that's exactly what happened. Originally trying to approximate a real acoustic kick drum with simple analog synthesis, Roland engineers implemented a simple decay control for the kick drum. But the range of this control went way beyond the parameters of a "real" acoustic drum, allowing for a crazy-long low frequency wave that knocked down walls when greatly amplified. The urban legend goes that when digital drum machines like the LinnDrum and Oberheim DMX were released in the '80s, musicians dumped off TR-808s like yesterday's news, and many of them ended up in the hands of up-and-coming New York and Detroit dance and hip-hop producers. Upon discovery of "the boom," they made use of the 808 in ways its creators never intended.

The 808 kick was all the rage in early-80s hip-hop projects, such as LL Cool J's "Rock the Bells," the Beastie Boys' entire *License to Ill* album, L'Trimm's "Cars with the Boom," Sir Mix-a-Lot's "Baby Got Back," and countless others. Later the boom invaded techno, most notably with the Prodigy, and right up to the present with the Black Eyed Peas; their track "Don't Phunk with My Heart" carries the 808 sound right into 2006.

The 808's kick drum utilized something called a "bridged T-network" for sound generation. To simplify, it's basically a resonant filter network hanging on the edge of sine wave feedback, triggered by a little click of audio. We can re-create this by taking a low-pass filter and cranking the resonance (sometimes called "emphasis") all the way up. This makes our filter become an oscillator.

You can use almost any virtual analog software or hardware synth. I used Native Instruments' Pro-53, which works great. Here's why I say *almost* any: Different virtual (and real analog) synths have different filter implementations. Some are more prone to oscillation than others, so some won't "ring" enough to give the kind of solid tone we need to boom in the room. You might have to try a couple.

With that in mind, let's start. We'll skip the oscillator section altogether, because our filter is doing the oscillating for us. Set the cutoff frequency very low, almost to zero. As mentioned, we'll take the resonance control and turn it to its maximum setting. *Make sure the volume is down, because this can sometimes be louder than you expect.* Now we want to modulate the cutoff frequency with the filter envelope. Since our filter is really an oscillator here, we're using the filter envelope to sweep the pitch a little, so the pitch falls. The attack should be zero, decay about two seconds, sustain zero, and release about two seconds as well. Now slowly bring up the filter's envelope amount so you can hear the envelope sweeping the pitch. The pitch only needs to fall a little bit, and we want to keep the whole thing pretty low; this is a kick drum here! Bring up the keyboard tracking as well so that the pitch of the filter gets higher as you ascend up the keyboard. This way you'll get different pitches of boom, which is really cool for drum-and-bass styles.

You can set the amplitude envelope to your liking. Attack should be zero, which usually will impart a slight "click" to the top of the sound. That's a good thing for a drum. Decay should of course be long, two or more seconds. Sustain is up to you. If you want it to sound just like a drum, leave it low, but higher values will let you "play" the kick by holding down notes. Release should be long as well.

My "secret weapon" is putting an overdrive or mild distortion plug-in on the sound. This will really help your kick to cut through. Logic's stock "Overdrive" plug works great. You can get a lot of great variations by playing with the overdrive controls. Just go easy on the distortion so you don't lose the bass. You still want it to sound like a kick! Just watch the level of sub bass so you don't blow anything up. You can download my Pro-53 patch and some sound at www.celebutantemusic/keybmag or at www.keyboard-mag.com. Bada-bing, bada-BOOM!

Roll your own monster 808 kick sound with an analog synth or soft synth such as Native Instruments Pro-53

A little overdrive will give your 808 kick a huge boost. Here are the settings using Apple Logic Pro's Overdrive plug-in.

RETURN OF THE BLING

Pulse-Width Modulation Will Make Your Synths Shine

Once again, I'm faced with the tricky task of using words to describe a classic analog synth flavor. This month's installment details one my favorite analog synth patches, sort of a rich analog bling. Pling? Maybe fling?

Let's make this easier by name-dropping some tracks. The first song that made me aware of this sound was the Fixx's spooky anthem "Red Skies at Night"; it's in every verse playing the melodies. You can hear a similar sound in the lead melodies of the Thompson Twins' "Lies," and also in the choruses of Berlin's "Pleasure Victim."

If you've spent any time with classic analog polysynths such as the Sequential Circuits Prophet-5, Roland Jupiter-8, or the Oberheim OB series, you'll note that they deliver serious low-end punch. But they can sound a little thin in the higher registers, even with two oscillators. However, the judicious use of pulse-width modulation does a pretty nice job of simulating the wobbling pitch undulation of a chorus effect and thickens things nicely.

Like my old-school New Wave heroes, I make use of this sound on my Prophet-5 quite a bit, but you can use all manner of virtual analog synths to simulate it. The synth must have two oscillators with pulse-width modulation capabilities, aka PWM. For this example, I'll be using Arturia's Prophet-V virtual synth in the Prophet-5-only mode. This instrument sounds awesome!

We'll start with our oscillators. Set both to the variable pulse wave setting (usually the square wave setting). Set the initial pitch so that the oscillators play an octave apart from one another. They should be detuned as well; about 12 cents apart is good. Now comes the important part: modulating the pulse width. Modulating the wha . . . ? Perhaps an explanation is in order.

If you've ever used the square wave setting and twisted the knob that says "pulse width," you've noticed a dramatic timbral change occurring. When the pulse width is at either extreme, the rectangular wave becomes very narrow, as does the sound, making for a handy analogy. If you twist it too far, the waveform becomes so narrow that the sound disappears entirely. Toward the middle of its range, the wave comes closer to a perfect square shape, and takes on a full, fat, flutey tone. If you continuously twist the pulse width knob back and forth, you get a really pleasant timbral animation, as well as a little bit of pitch wobble. You also get a tired hand—and only have one hand to play notes with. But thanks to the wonder of the low-frequency oscillator, or LFO, we don't need to wear out our hands. Using an LFO set to a simple triangle wave to control the pulse width, we can mimic the effect of continuously turning the pulse-width knob back and forth. Christmas!

Now that we've cleared up the pulse-width modulation business, set the LFO to a triangle wave and route it to the pulse width of both oscillators. Set the LFO speed to something pretty quick; I set mine to 4.85 Hz. If you're using any sort of real or virtual Prophet-5, you'll need to turn up the mod wheel close to full up and leave it to set the modulation depth. Otherwise, turn up the depth knob as far as possible without the sound disappearing. You may need to play with the initial pulse-width setting, but typically you'll want it in the middle of its range.

Set the level of both oscillators to full tilt in the mixer section, and then proceed to the filter. We want a standard low-pass-type filter with cutoff frequency in a middle setting. Turn the resonance up to around 25 percent for some extra mids. We'll set the filter envelope to a guitar-type shape and turn the envelope amount parameter about halfway up. Attack should be zero, decay about 1,000 ms, sustain level low, and release relatively long (about 1,500 ms). We want an instantaneous peak when notes are struck that fades out and rings when we release notes. This makes for beautiful cascading melodies and arpeggios, especially when you break out the delay and reverb. Moving on to the volume envelope, simply duplicate the settings detailed above for the filter envelope. Feel free to cheat and apply some chorus and delay, but I think you'll find the patch pretty full without any outside help. You can download my Arturia Pro-V patch and some audio samples at www.celebutantemusic/keybmag or at www.keyboardmag.com. Bling, pling, fling indeed!

Arturia's Prophet-V is a wicked hybrid emulating Sequential Circuits' Prophet-5 and Prophet VS synths.

TEMPTED BY THE ORGANS OF OTHERS

Create Classic Tone Wheel Organ Sounds, Analog-Style

The other day I was checking out the video for Squeeze's classic tune "Tempted" and couldn't help but notice that Paul Carrack was playing the organ sounds on a Prophet-5 synth (and a coveted "rev. 2" version at that). My rational brain told me that in all likelihood the "organ" I heard was really a Hammond B-3, played through a Leslie rotating speaker, as you can hear the Leslie speaker speeding up and slowing down throughout the track. But maybe, just maybe, I conjectured, this was really a Prophet on the recording, creating glorious organ noises. So I turned on my Prophet, and let it warm up for 20 minutes (things are very atonal if you skip this step), and set about making the world's most authentic analog synth B-3 organs!

On the surface, analog synths (and their virtual equivalents) don't appear to be very good candidates for creating tone wheel organ patches, but I recently stumbled upon a simple trick that makes for great organ sounds. But first, a little primer.

A tone wheel organ contains many gear-like metal wheels. These are rotated in proximity to a magnetic pickup and create a series of simple sine wave-like waveforms with very few harmonic overtones. A single sine wave contains only a fundamental tone with no harmonics and is a very simple and basic (read: boring) tone. Most acoustic and electronic instruments have complex and distinctive harmonic overtones that make them interesting to the ear. This sonic "signature" is why a flugelhorn sounds different than a viola, for example.

In order to generate interesting tones, tone wheel organs combined multiple intervals, including octaves, fifths, and major thirds. This resulted in an early form of additive synthesis. So ideally, we need many sine wave oscillators to accurately mimic a tone wheel organ. The problem is that most classic analog synth architectures contain just two or three oscillators, hardly enough to compete with the Hammond, which effectively has nine oscillators. Or are they?

Remember when we said that the Hammond's tone wheels create simple sine waves with few harmonics? The average analog synth sawtooth or pulse wave is chock-full of harmonic overtones, greatly reducing the need for many oscillators. And here's where the simple trick I mentioned comes into play. If we tune one of the oscillators up in octaves and fifths from the root, we get the whole harmonic series, shifted up, offering a whole other set of interesting overtones to spice up our organ emulation. Let's get down the nitty-gritty and get organ-ized.

For this example, I made use of Native Instrument's awesome new virtual synth Massive (say it loudly, with authority), but you can create great organs with almost any two-oscillator virtual analog. Starting with the oscillator section, select the variable pulse wave for both oscillators. I used the "SquSw II" setting on Massive, as it doesn't have a standard pulse wave. You can tune the second oscillator up a fifth above oscillator one as mentioned, but for super-high organ harmonics, I tuned it up an octave and a fifth above oscillator one. This really offers a nice harmonic spread (you can even go two octaves and a fifth). From here, set the filter to low-pass (24 dB if there's an option) and turn the resonance up about three-quarters. Stop before the filter starts whistling on its own. This will take some trial and error, but set the filter cutoff frequency about 40 percent open. If it's too bright, it won't sound anything like an organ, so be careful. Set the volume envelope to a simple on/off shape; instant attack, instant decay, sustain full up, and release very fast. Set the LFO to add an equal amount of triangle wave vibrato to both oscillators. Moderation is the key.

You may need to add some EQ for realism. A little low-end cut and maybe a midrange bump around 500 Hz can help. And if you have a plug-in that simulates a Leslie speaker, turn that guy on!

Since tone wheel organs offer a lot of variation, here are some tips to mix it up:

• Try different pulse-width settings for the oscillator waveforms.
• Adjust the levels of the oscillators relative to each other; turning the fundamental way down and leaving the octave-and-a-fifth oscillator loud makes for great vintage sounds.
• Carefully tweak the filter's cutoff and resonance controls for mellower or more aggressive tonalities.

You can download my Massive B-3 patch plus some audio samples at www.celebutantemusic/keybmag or at www.keyboardmag.com. 'Til next month, avoid temptation and wail on those wicked organ tones!

Tone wheel organ emulations are a walk in the park for Native Instrument's powerhouse virtual synth, Massive.

EVERYTHING IN ITS RHODES PLACE

How to Make Dreamy Radiohead Pianos

Ever hear a synth sound that immediately grabbed you by the ears and made you wonder what it was? And when you figured it out, you realized it was so simple that you smacked yourself for not coming up with it yourself? I sure have, and Radiohead's "Everything in Its Right Place" is one those songs. From their mysterious *Kid A* CD, this was the kickoff track that made a lot of folks wonder where the heck they were going on this deep, dreamy disc.

At first, "Everything's" main figure appears to be a Rhodes electric piano. But on closer listen, it's a little too robotic and electronic-sounding to be a real Rhodes (the other giveaway is the lack of high-frequency tine overtones, but more on that later). Lucky for us, at the very end of the track, Radiohead kindly gives away the secret: By opening the filter wide and tweaking with the resonance, it becomes clear that it's an analog polysynth. On Radiohead's *Meeting People Is Easy* DVD, you can see Johnny Greenwood in the studio manning a Sequential Circuits Prophet-5, so I'm guessing that's what they used. Making the patch is deceptively easy, but I'll throw in a few tricks to spice it up.

Almost any polyphonic virtual analog synth will do; there isn't too much crazy voodoo involved. We're going to use a one-oscillator patch with the waveform set to a narrow pulse wave. If you have variable pulse-width control, set it almost as narrow as it will go, about 10–20 percent. You may need to tweak this later on. You'll want to set the oscillator an octave or two down to get everything in its right range. The audio samples on www.keyboardmag.com should help you in the fine-tuning process (if not, I make house calls).

We'll use a low-pass filter (24 dB if you have the option), with the cutoff frequency almost all the way down. Set the keyboard tracking close to all the way up, so the sound gets gradually brighter as you ascend the keyboard. And we'll use an envelope generator to gently shape the filter cutoff frequency; this is usually governed by the "envelope amount" knob. Set the filter envelope for zero attack, long decay, almost full sustain level, and a long release (about five seconds). Now gradually bring up the envelope amount knob until the notes have a little bit of shape. This is a very dark sound we're after, so don't be afraid to keep it mellow and turn up the volume; dang, I sound like a hippie! The amplitude envelope should be set to match the filter envelope closely: long and dreamy.

Here's where the "outside trickery" comes into play. If you listen to the track, the sound is very in your face and wide. We'll accomplish the "in your face" part with lots of compression. You'll want to use the warmest, biggest compressor in your arsenal; I used the Waves Renaissance compressor. Now we need the wide part. Go back for a moment: We could thicken things up by using a two-oscillator patch and detuning the oscillators slightly. But instead, I recommend sending the sound to a nice, wide stereo chorus or doubler effect in your mixer's bus section. Why? Dual-oscillator synth patches have a different tonality than chorused single-oscillator sounds, that's why! It's hard to describe, but it's a little starker, which is what we're after. Experiment, see for yourself, and add this to your bag of programming tricks. I used Logic's Spreader effect here. You can also add some quarter-note delay for fun. The delay time is about 485 ms, and if you're programming it in your sequencer, the track is in 10/4 time! Very crafty they are.

One more super-fly trick: If you'd like to mix in a dash of Rhodes authenticity, you can use a second oscillator to re-create the super-high-pitched Rhodes tine noise. You can use a thin pulse wave or a triangle wave, and set the interval at two octaves, nine half steps, and 50 cents above the main oscillator (this is the same as 33 half steps and 50 cents). You'll want to fine-tune the mix level. You might also need to open up the cutoff frequency to let that little guy through.

You can download my Logic ES2 patches plus audio samples of all this madness at www.celebutantemusic/keybmag or at www.keyboardmag.com. Until we meet again, keep those electric pianos in their right place!

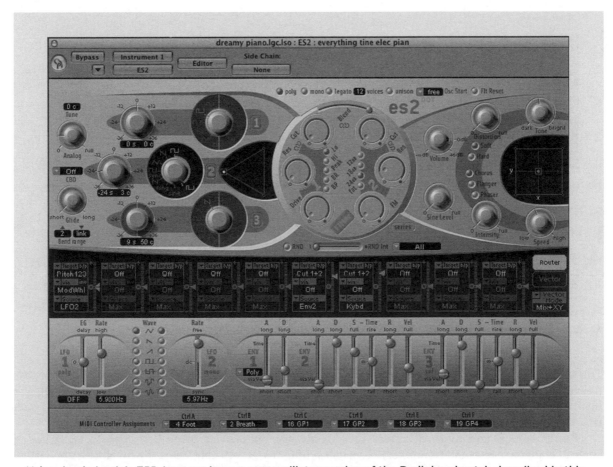

Using Apple Logic's ES2, here we have a one-oscillator version of the Radiohead patch described in this article. But if you look closely at oscillator three on the bottom, you'll see the interval setting for the optional high-tine noise.

SYNTH PLAYERS JUST WANNA HAVE FUN

How to Bring Back Those Blippy '80s Filter Tones

MAY 2007

Between gigs, I'm often called upon to re-create famous synth tracks for cover bands. This can be pretty fun, and often it brings sounds to my attention that I might not have otherwise noticed. Recently I was asked to re-create the synth tracks for Cyndi Lauper's 1983 MTV megahit, "Girls Just Wanna Have Fun." The main chords are played on a simple vintage Vox organ with a syncopated echo, but the solo section contains a blippy, vaguely Caribbean-tinged synth patch, courtesy of a Roland Juno-60 (Lionel Richie, Kid Creole, and "Weekend at Bernie's" were really rockin' that Caribbean vibe in the '80s). The patch almost sounds like electronic steel drums; it's also reminiscent of the signature sound in Gershon Kingsley's novelty Moog hit "Popcorn."

The secret to the "Girls" solo is not using the synth's oscillators at all. Instead we'll crank up a low-pass filter's resonance control (sometimes called "emphasis" or "Q") to maximum. This will cause the filter to resonate and create a pure sine wave, which is traditionally tough for standard voltage-controlled oscillators or their virtual synth equivalents.

Ready to twist some virtual knobs? To illustrate how simple this patch is to make, I made use of Logic's relatively basic (and Juno-like) ES1 virtual synth, though you can create it with almost any virtual synth that has a resonating filter.

As mentioned, this patch doesn't need standard oscillators, so make sure the oscillator volumes are set to zero. Move over to the filter, and if it has the option, set it for 24-dB-per-octave, low-pass mode. Before we go any further, turn the master volume down, because things can get loud here! Now that we're at a safe level, dial the resonance control all the way up; you should hear a pure, basic sine wave. Now we need to tune this guy. The procedure will vary a bit depending on what synth you're using, but look for a "keyboard tracking" control, or some variation thereof. On some synths, it's one of the filter controls; on others, you may need to go to the modulation matrix and route "keyboard" to the "cutoff frequency." If your filter has this built in, full-up typically corresponds to setting the frequency to track standard half-step scales properly. As an aside, the "keyboard tracking" control is usually used so that cutoff frequency increases as the oscillator's pitch is ascending, effectively keeping the brightness of the tone constant across the keyboard. But since we're using the filter as a tone source, the tracking control is actually in-suring that the tone is a proper equal-tempered scale. The easiest way to make sure you're tracking the keyboard correctly is to play octaves. If they play in tune, all is well. If the upper note is flat, turn up the tracking amount. If the upper note is sharp, turn the tracking control down. If you can't get them in tune at all, congratulations, you own a real vintage analog synth; get 'em as close as you can!

Once you have the octaves playing in tune, the filter cutoff control will act as a "master tuning" control. Hit a note and play it against another synth to tune it, or better yet, play into a guitar tuner (I have a mixer aux out plugged into a guitar tuner that's on at all times; you won't believe how handy this is until you try it!). For "Girls Just Wanna Have Fun," you'll want the keyboard tuned in a relatively high register.

Now that everything's in tune, we'll set up a simple ADSR envelope. Attack will be instant; decay should be really quick for the blip, about 40 ms; no sustain; and make the release the same as decay. Many virtual synths will emit an audible pop at the beginning of the sound, so you may need to add a millisecond or two to the attack time to quell the click.

Now we're pretty much set. For a proper '80s "Yo, check out my sweet new digital reverb" effect, load this sound up with gated reverb. And if any of you have used a Roland Juno-6/60/106 synth, you'll know that the built-in chorus switch was in the "on" position at all times, so pop some chorus on too.

You can download my Logic ES1 patch plus some audio samples of me banging on them black keys at www.celebutantemusic/keybmag or at www.keyboardmag.com. Synth players, we wanna . . . wanna have fun, synth players . . .

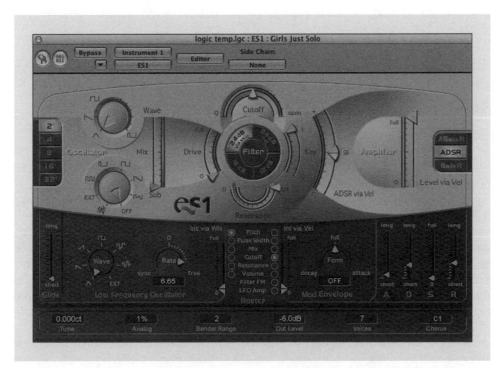

Here's the "resonating filter" patch in Apple Logic Pro's ES1. Remember to turn the oscillator volume levels down in the mixer section.

THEREMINS FROM SPACE

Creating Authentic Theremin Tones

By now, just about every electronic music aficionado is familiar with the haunting tone of Leon Theremin's 1920s-era "thereminvox," better known as the theremin. For those not in the know, the theremin was one of the first electronic instruments. Using a simple "heterodyning" oscillator (basically a variation on radio interference), the instrument had two metal antennae extending vertically and horizontally. By means of proximity, the player's hands controlled volume with one antenna and pitch with the other. With no concrete pitch reference, performing music that's in tune on the theremin is a challenge mastered by few. These days, the theremin is still alive and well, most notably those produced by Moog Music and performed upon by virtuosos such as Pamelia Kurstin, a supremely gifted modern-day thereminist.

Though there were a few notable classical theremin players (most notably virtuoso Clara Rockmore), the theremin inadvertently became the instrument of choice in cheesy '40s and '50s alien invasion flicks, usually warbling away with a lot of reverb, evoking faraway worlds. I'm not sure who decided this was what faraway worlds actually sound like, but only time will tell!

If you want to hear the theremin in action, check out www.thereminvox.com, which features a rich collection of audio examples, as well as some fascinating history (Russian inventor Leon Thermin lived a pretty colorful life). Led Zeppelin's Jimmy Page used one, somewhat atonally, in "Whole Lotta Love." The classic alien flick *The Day the Earth Stood Still* features the theremin, as well as the more recent Tim Burton films *Ed Wood* and *Mars Attacks.* But seeing Portishead's Adrian Utley playing convincing theremin lines on a Minimoog on their superlative *Roseland NYC Live* DVD really got me into faking the theremin funk—check out track one, "Humming."

For those of us who don't have the time to explore faraway galaxies or learn a difficult new instrument, let's make a nifty re-creation of the theremin sound using a virtual analog modeling synth. Almost any virtual analog synth will do. The only important requirements are a mono mode and portamento (also known as glide), so we can properly imitate the smoothly gliding pitches that occur as you move your hands through the air near a real theremin. For this month's example, I used Arturia's fabulous new Jupiter-8V.

We'll only need one oscillator, set to a sawtooth waveform. I set it to 8', but depending on your controller, you may need to set it higher; we want our theremin to get pretty screamin' high! The filter setting is simple yet crucial. Use a 24-dB-per-octave low-pass filter, and set the cutoff about halfway up. Resonance should be about half up as well; enough to have a "honky" horn-type tonality, but not so much that it sounds overly synth-like—*listen to the online samples to help fine-tune the settings.* Filter envelope and tracking should be turned off. The amplitude envelope (aka volume) should have a slow attack (around 600 ms), instant decay, sustain full up, and a pretty quick release (around 50 ms).

You've probably noticed that things don't sound very theremin-like yet. Here comes the mojo-voodoo stuff. First we need a bunch of vibrato. Route the low-frequency oscillator (LFO) to modulate the oscillator pitch. Select a sine or triangle waveform. Depth should be about a half step up and down; a good starting speed is around 6.0 Hz. Since real thereminists control vibrato by moving their hands like a violinist would, it's a great idea to assign vibrato speed to a real-time knob on your keyboard controller. Secondly, put the keyboard trigger in "mono" mode (so you play only one note at a time). Select "legato" if possible to prevent envelope retriggering. Now turn up the glide or portamento control so that pitches slowly glide up and down. Not only did I assign the glide speed to a real-time controller, but I assigned the amplitude envelope attack to a knob as well. As you can see, this is a sound that really begs to be played and manipulated, so work those controls for maximum fluidity and realism (or unrealism as the case may be!).

Finally, drench this guy in reverb or delay for full-on alien-attack authenticity. Keep that trusty ray gun at your side to fend off pesky aliens!

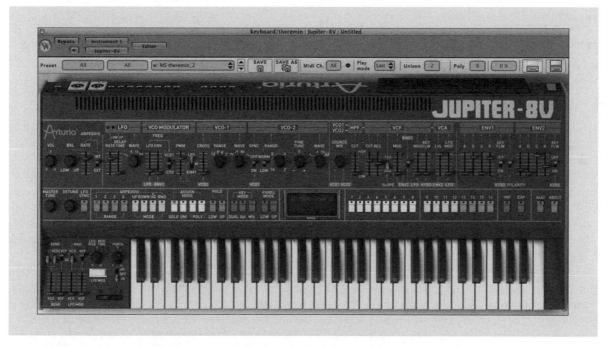

By control-clicking a parameter (or Apple key-clicking on Mac), you can easily assign real-time controls with Arturia's Jupiter-8V.

DOUBLE-WIDE
SUPER SIZE

Fat Velocity-Controlled Bass

What's the first thing you do when you check out the newest megaphonic super-monster synth of doom? Admit it, your fingers instinctively travel to the leftmost nether regions of the keys to check out some big, fat bass patches! Hey, I do it too. At least I've been able to cut down on the two-handed sixteenth-note riffs ("Hello, my name is Mitch and I'm a recovering industrialaholic"). So in this spirit, I give you, the bomb velocity-controlled bass. Of course, most synth bass patches have velocity-controlled volume, brightness, or some combination thereof programmed in. But we're going to take a slightly different approach, and it shall be fun.

The idea here is that instead of having a bass patch with the normal sharp attack and slow decay, we're going to create a sound with an organ-like on/off envelope, but with extreme velocity-controlled analog filter juiciness. But that's just part of the equation; we'll get to the rest in a bit. First here are some sonic reference points.

We'll start with the leadoff track from Depeche Mode's *Violator* disc, "World in My Eyes." This has to be some of the meanest synth bass ever recorded, courtesy of Alan Wilder's custom MIDI-fied Minimoog/Oberheim SEM rack. It's a mix of a couple parts, but you can clearly hear the different filter cutoff settings on each note. In a similar vein, the Sneaker Pimps' "Low Place Like Home" incorporates a slithery, gliding mono synth bass that leans heavy on the resonance. And the Crystal Method makes use of a similar heavy-on-the-glide, heavy-on-the-resonance type patch in the signature riff of "Busy Child."

So what of this velocity-controlled bass? Let's make the patch. I used Arturia's Minimoog V, an obvious choice for big-time bass, but you can use other virtual analog synths. Because of triggering and glide, some may not work as well as others, but the basic ideas will work. First, I used two oscillators split one octave apart, both with sawtooth waves selected. Detune them a wee bit for flavor. Moving to the filter, initial cutoff frequency should be very low; just enough so that a dark but audible sound comes through. Crank the resonance (or "emphasis" in Moogspeak) up to about 60 percent. Filter envelope amount should be zero. Amplitude envelope controls should have zero attack, zero decay, sustain full up, and release on zero. Ignore the release if you're using a Minimoog clone.

Now we'll transform our relatively boring bass patch into something fun. In the modulation routing section, set the source to velocity and the destination to filter cutoff. Now set the amount to around 50–75 percent. You'll need to experiment, but when you play light the bass should be super dark, and when you really whack it you should hear cutting sawtooths. The idea is to avoid turning the mod depth up too high; otherwise, all of your harder velocities will make for full brightness, thereby compromising your dull-to-bright dynamic range.

Now make sure the sound is in mono mode, i.e., you can only play one key at a time. Different synths use different nomenclature, but just look for the section that has a poly, mono, or "number of voices" setting and set it for mono or one voice. Most synths also have options for the mono mode, including retrigger and legato modes. Retrigger means the envelopes will start at the beginning of their cycles with every key press, whereas legato mode restarts the envelopes only when *all* keys have been released and a new key is pressed. Set this to legato. Finally, since we're in mono mode, most synths have a switch to give the high, low, or last note hit priority; set this to "last," i.e., the most recently hit note sounds.

Now it's all in how you play it. The fun thing is that you can hold your left hand down on a key and hit notes with your right hand at different velocities, radically altering the color of the bass tone. Try adding a heavy dose of glide, and you're all set to get busy, child! You can hear audio examples at www.keyboard-mag.com or at www.celebutantemusic/keybmag. Make sure to crank up the subs; tell your neighbors that the guy from the book said you had to!

Arturia's Minimoog V has a "hidden" control panel for mod routings, accessed by clicking the "Open" button in the upper-right corner. Check out all those extras!

DISTORTION OF DOOM

How to Get That Pedal to the Metal Synth Fuzz

AUGUST 2007

I have to admit it: I never really liked the idea of plugging a synth into a distortion pedal. Lots of folks have done it in varying contexts. But every time I busted out the Boss Super Overdrive that's been with me since 1983, something didn't feel right. But then I heard a couple of records that turned me around. First I heard Orgy's searing cover of the New Order classic "Blue Monday." Not too adventurous as cover versions go, but it had a great distorted bass guitar/synth/I-don't-know-what-it-is that sure sounded mean.

Then I discovered the band Deadsy, who used a similar sound, stripped and naked, all over their debut disc, *Commencement*. This was really killing me. Both Orgy and Deadsy were primarily produced and recorded at the same studio; these guys all seemed to know each other. To cut a long story short, I befriended one of the guitarists in Deadsy, and I had my answer. The sound I was hearing wasn't a guitar or bass, but in fact a Roland JP-8080 synth patched into a Boss Hyperfuzz pedal. Actually, two of 'em, for stereo. My friend Carlton was controlling all this with a Z-Tar MIDI controller for a sort of futuristic guitar vibe, which I later experienced myself when I filled in on a handful of live shows.

Since then I've made a practice of using this big, growling tone in a number of production styles. What's great is that it sounds sort of like power chords, but it's deeper, darker, and fuzzier, so it's nice for filling in the space between bass and electric guitar. Of course there are a ton of ways to distort a synth, but I've found some really neat ones, and some secrets along the way that I'll share. Aren't you lucky?

Let's make the synth patch. This is simple, and as long as you've got a virtual synth with two oscillators, just about anything will do the job. Select sawtooth waveforms on both oscillators. We'll make the first oscillator the "root" note, and then set the interval on the second oscillator a perfect fifth up; this is equivalent to seven half steps up. The filter should be the standard low-pass variety. Cutoff frequency will need to be really low, so the distortion doesn't sound like a total buzz saw, but it's best to play with the setting once you set up the distortion. The same goes for the resonance setting. We don't want any filter envelope, so make sure the filter envelope intensity is zeroed out. The amplitude envelope should be a straight on/off affair: attack at zero, decay at zero, sustain full up, and release almost zero.

Now we have a relatively dull one-finger power-chord patch. Here's where you'll want to plug this guy into a distortion device. Now the fuzz box of choice can make all the difference between blah and blazam, so choose your weapon carefully, rock soldier. What I've found is that the best sounding fuzz boxes usually don't live inside a computer. And the more extreme, the better. Overdrive or tube screamer-type stomp boxes are usually intended for guitarists to beef up their tone a bit when plugging into an already distorted guitar amp—not what we're after here. Fuzz boxes aren't meant to preserve the natural tone of the $4,000 Les Paul you just got; they're meant to destroy it. The aforementioned Boss Hyperfuzz is such a device, and it sounds great for power-chord synth mayhem. I've found most octave-fuzz devices sound really awesome in this setting. The venerable ProCo Rat makes a neat synth distorter too. And my secret weapon: the Danelectro French Toast octave-fuzz. Super cheap, super noisy. Sounds amazing with the octave switch on!

When using stomp boxes, keep in mind that their inputs are designed for electric guitars, which have meager output, so turn things down real quiet. Remember to experiment with the synth's filter cutoff and resonance controls; you'll be amazed at how dark the filter can get and still achieve great fuzz tones. Another neat trick: Plug the fuzz box into a real amp or an amp simulator. No crazy gain settings; use a moderate crunch, such as on Fender Twin or Bassman models. And finally, try some stereo chorusing or doubling to widen up your wall of fuzz, always at the end of the chain; chorus plugged into distortion is bad ugly, not good ugly. Until next month, rattle those fillings with the rawk!

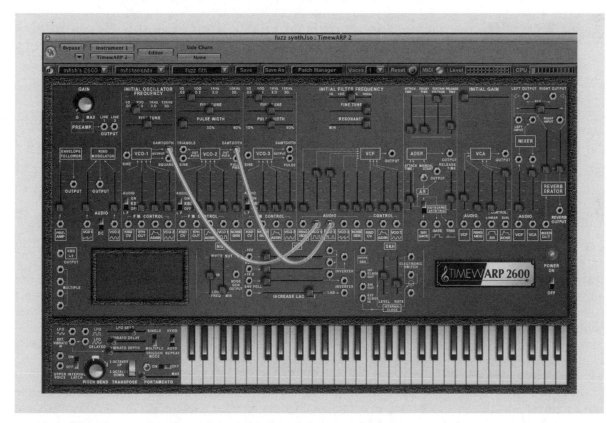

For the megafuzz, I used Way Out Ware's TimewARP 2600 synth. Notice the virtual patch cords needed for sawtooth waves with oscillator one and two. Dangly!

JUST UNTIL THE SWELLING GOES DOWN

Prescription: Perilous Prophet Pads

I n the last couple of years, the venerable Sequential Circuits Prophet-5 has been re-created virtually in a number of guises, notably with Native Instruments' Pro-53 and Arturia's Prophet-V, the latter of which combines an emulation of the original Prophet with Sequential's later Prophet VS digital/analog hybrid synth. This month I'd like to share a pretty cool Prophet patch from my personal stash. It's featured on the track "Transactions" from my CD, *Nightlife*, which I would, uh, never blatantly promote here. (Hint: www.celebusite. com . . . must . . . not . . . self-promote. . . .)

It's a spooky pad that slowly swells in from nothing and then ends rather abruptly. As a result, it sounds a little backward, since the envelopes are set in the opposite way of most piano or guitar-type patches. I also did some trickery to make it very wide and stereo-ized, which is a technique you can apply to other sounds. You can hear it in the samples I've posted online at www.keyboardmag.com or at www.celebutantemusic.com/keybmag. I created this patch using Native Instruments' Pro-53. You don't need a Prophet (real or virtual) to do it; just about any two-oscillator polysynth with pulse-width modulation will do. Use whatever you've got, friends.

Let's start with two oscillators at equal volume and set the octaves to a middle range with both in the same register. Use the fine-pitch knob to detune oscillator B by a fair amount, about 30 cents. It should sound kind of seasick, but not so out of tune that it's unplayable. Select the square waveform for both oscillators as well. On some synths this will be called PWM; you want the one with variable pulse-width (some synths have a fixed square wave). Now we want to route the low-frequency oscillator (LFO) to modulate the pulse width of the square wave. That's a scary-sounding sentence, but all it means is that instead of turning the pulse-width knob back and forth for timbral animation, we're going to have our friend the LFO do it automatically for us. Moving to the LFO section, select a triangle waveform, and set the speed to about 6 Hz. You can match it up to the audio examples if your synth doesn't show the exact speed. If you're using Pro-53 in Logic, you can select the Editor page in the plug window to accurately display the knob increment values. Now we want to route the LFO to control pulse width. On a Prophet, you'll go to the Wheel-Mod section, select PW A and PW B, and then crank the mod wheel up about two-thirds (I'm referring to the virtual mod wheel next to the keyboard in the plug-in interface, not the actual mod wheel on your MIDI controller).

Moving over to the filter, we want a low-pass with the cutoff frequency about 40 percent open or less; we're going to use the filter envelope to do most of our cutoff control. Resonance should be at about 20 percent just to focus the sound a bit. You'll want to experiment with the filter envelope times depending on the tempo of the song, but for my 139-bpm tune, I had a relatively long attack and decay, sustain almost full up, and zero release time. The really important thing is to crank up the envelope amount knob so that the envelope takes the sound from semi-dull to wide open. Keyboard tracking can be at 100 percent. The amplitude envelope will look similar to the filter, but you'll want to speed up the attack; most of our "swell" effect is coming from the filter sweep, not an actual volume change.

The PWM and wide oscillator detune should have things sounding pretty fat, but we're still in mono. For a nice stereo-ization, I used an aux send to add a 10 ms delay. I panned the Pro-53 patch a little to the right, and the delay hard right. Now things are big. Just don't let the swelling get out of hand.

One quirk of the Prophet-5 (and its virtual brethren, such as Native Instruments Pro-53, shown here) is that the mod wheel just next to the keyboard has to be up for LFO modulation to work, so remember to turn that guy up.

COMBO COMMANDO

Bring in the Wheeze with Combo Organ Cheese

When most folks think of rock 'n' roll organ sounds, it's usually the hulking Hammond that comes to mind. But with the innovation of transistors in the '60s replacing hot and heavy vacuum tubes, came the compact and affordable combo organ with a sonic squelch all its own. Back then, if you couldn't afford a Hammond (or didn't have friends to move it), a combo organ was the only choice. Their dulcet cheese-o-rific tones were heard all over the radio in tunes such as "House of the Rising Sun" by the Animals and Question Mark and the Mysterians' classic "96 Tears," as well as many Doors hits. As the '60s psychedelic era faded, so did the combo organ craze, effectively mothballing most of these instruments. But everything comes in cycles, right? Thusly, the New Wave movement brought back the humble weeze of the combo organ with artists such as the B-52s, Elvis Costello, and Blondie crankin' 'em up again. And more recently, retro organs have been used by artists such as Smashmouth on their hit, "Walking on the Sun," as well as Pulp, and the Kaiser Chiefs.

Compact transistor organs utilized a "divide-down" network with an oscillator for each of the top 12 chromatic notes of the scale. The oscillators then ran through circuitry generating pitches in the appropriate lower octaves to cover the entire range of the keyboard. This technique saw continued usage in many string synths, organs, and electronic pianos. Most compact organs also featured a drawbar system where different octaves (as well as intervals) could be layered together to make more complex tones. The drawbars looked a whole lot like a Hammond organ, but they sounded completely different, giving the little transistorized organs their unique plasticky sound.

The tone generation in a compact organ is relatively archaic by today's standards, so with some clever tweakery, we can coax some pretty authentic cheese from modern virtual polysynths. For this month's example, I used Arturia's big bad Roland Jupiter-8V, but most of the programming can easily be adapted to others. Start out by setting both oscillators to square waves. If there's a pulse-width control, set it in the middle to achieve the "squarest" tone (i.e., the thickest sound). Now set the oscillators one octave apart. Make sure the fine tuning is set to zero; we don't want any beating or chorusing between the oscillators; otherwise, it will sound like a modern synth and destroy our cheese-organ illusion. Now we need some vibrato! We'll do this by using a low-frequency oscillator (LFO) set to a sine or triangle wave to modulate the pitch. I set the depth to .035, which is a bit less than a quarter tone in each direction. I set the speed to 6.22 Hz, fast enough to be frenetic, but not fast enough to sound like a synth.

The filter settings are pretty simple. Open the cutoff almost all they way; keep it down a little because everything in the '60s was a little lo-fi! We won't need any resonance or filter envelope at all. If you're using the Jupiter or another synth with an additional high-pass filter, use it to filter out a lot of the lows, again helping our lo-fi illusion. If your synth only has a low-pass filter, don't fret. Just add an EQ plug-in set to high-pass after the synth in your mixer, and knock down everything below 500 Hz. Think thin! Make sure the volume envelope is set to a simple organ "on/off" shape: attack at zero, decay at zero, sustain full up, and a quick release.

That's it. For more fun, try adding a small amount of overdrive or an amp simulator for some grit; I used the Jupiter-8V's built-in distortion insert effect between the filter and amp sections, but this is a unique feature. A regular plug-in after the synth will work just as well. Be sure to experiment with the oscillators' octave settings and the pulse width of the waveforms for thicker and thinner tones. You can download the Jupiter-8V patch and check out audio examples at www.keyboardmag.com or at www.celebutantemusic/keybmag. Until next month, please pass the combo organ tones and cheese!

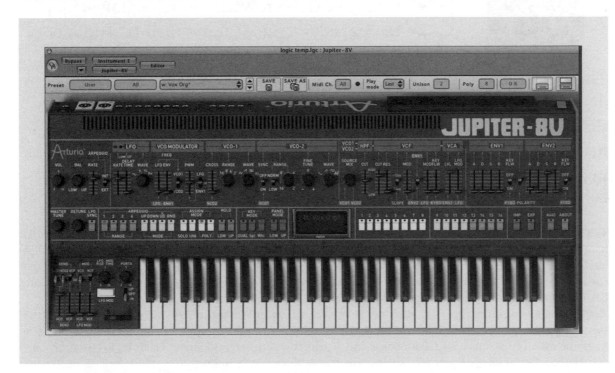

The tiny button at the upper right of the Aurturia Jupiter 8V (above the power switch) allows access to the effects section. I used this to insert a distortion effect between the filter and amp sections.

I THINK I FOUND THE FUNK

Six Tips to Help You Dial in Bernie Worrell's Rump-Shakin' Minimoog Bass

Bernie Worrell not only found the funk, he invented it. When folks around the globe talk of the legendary, funky, fatter-than-fat Minimoog bass, Bernie and his Mini are the team they speak of. Bob Moog couldn't have had a clue that this was where his synths would go, but did they ever! It's safe to say that a lot of the magic lies in Bernie's soulful fingers, but we're here to help nail that Minimoog bass magic no matter if you've got Bernie's amazing chops or not. Here are some tips on nailing the sound of Parliament's classic jam "Flash Light."

1. The ladder filter. Much of the Minimoog's revered "fat" sound is a result of its unique "ladder" filter, named for its sets of paired transistors. The ladder filter is used in most Moog synths, old and new. Analog synths from Studio Electronics as well as many modular systems utilize this design, and it's a direct road to the land of the big bass. If you don't have a real-deal analog synth, the Arturia Minimoog V and GForce Minimonsta virtual analog soft synths will get you pretty darn close.

2. Clean is for wimps. One neat Mini trait is its subtle inherent distortion. If you're using a clean virtual synth, try a little overdrive; just a bit for flavor. Careful if you use stomp boxes, as these sometimes reduce the amount of sub-bass frequencies, and we don't want that! And since "Flash Light" was recorded way before digital anything, surely analog tape was adding a little mojo.

3. It's hip to be square. The "Flash Light" bass sound is all about big fat square waves. Square wave bass sounds can sound huge when done right, but can get sterile if they're too clean. Try out tip No. 2 to avoid this!

4. Put some glide in yo' stride. Make sure to use the glide or portamento knob to add slides between notes. This is how to achieve Bernie's famous "woooo" sound; crank up the glide and do some serious smears and slides up and down the keys. (Hint: don't do this with the back of your hand while wearing black nail polish. Trust me on this.) Funky portamento playing takes some practice. It's a good idea to play with the portamento knob, cranking it up for crazy slides and effects, and laying off for straight-up bass jams.

5. Goin' around the bend. Make sure to pitch-bend those notes in combination with the glide for extra funk. This is where modern synths actually work better than old ones; you'll want to set the pitch-bend range to exactly a whole step, which makes playing far easier than older synths, which often had a somewhat arbitrary (and non-adjustable) pitch-bend range.

6. You say tomato, I say legato. Unlike polysynths, Minimoog keyboards are single-triggering by design. Huh? This means that if you play one note while holding another, the envelopes don't retrigger. Think of plucking a string on a guitar, then sliding your finger around on the string. Simply drag your fingers a bit when playing (i.e., don't let up on old notes 'til you've hit a new one) when you want the legato sound, and lift off old notes quickly when you want to hear the attacks. If you're using a newer synth, set the keyboard assign mode to "mono" and "legato."

Now that we've covered the basics, lets hit some specifics. For my samples, I used Arturia's Minimoog V plug-in. If you have three oscillators available, use 'em all, set to square waves. Tune oscillator one and two to the same octave (32' on a Mini), and oscillator three up one octave (16' on a Mini). Detune them a little, but keep them pretty tight; I tuned oscillators two and three up and down by 1.5 percent, respectively. Back off on the volume of oscillator three a bit compared to one and two. Moving to the filter, cutoff frequency should be about 60–70 percent open, resonance ("emphasis" in Moog-speak) all the way down, and filter envelope ("contour" in Moog-speak) up just a bit for a tiny punch on the note attacks. Filter envelope attack should be zero, decay about 500 ms, and sustain level about 20 percent. Amplitude envelope attack and decay should be set for zero, and sustain level full up. Release should be zero as well. I've put samples of the sound in different stages online to help dial 'em in.

You can download my Arturia Minimoog V patch and check out "guided audio tours" for creating this patch at www.keyboardmag.com or at www.celebutantemusic/keybmag. Keep it funky brother!

On the Arturia Minimoog V, the "LEGATO ON" switch is above the pitch and mod wheels. The original Minimoog synth was permanently set to "legato" mode.

BLIZZARD OF DON

Don Airey's Chilling "Mr. Crowley" Intro

Back in 1981, the meanest, evilest slab of "'evy meh-ul" was Ozzy Osbourne's Blizzard of Ozz. Emerging from the ashes of Black Sabbath, Ozzy was back on his feet with a new band featuring the soon-to-be-legendary young guitarist Randy Rhoads. But Ozzy had another secret weapon in virtuoso key-man Don Airey, a veteran of Ritchie Blackmore's Rainbow.

Throughout his early musical career, Ozzy's music frequently referenced his fascination with Satanism and the occult, and never more clearly than in "Mr. Crowley," a song about the life of notorious British devil-worshipper Aleister Crowley. Keyboardist Don Airey whipped up a spooky, plodding intro consisting of a massive cathedral organ, ominous Moog bass, and some faux-choir for good measure, recalling Rick Wakeman's equally haunting "Catherine of Aragon" from the classic *The Six Wives of Henry VIII*. This month we'll re-create the elements of Don's dark sonic stew.

We'll work from the bottom up. First we'll need the fat Minimoog bass. Just to show that you don't necessarily need a Minimoog or an exact replica, I used Logic's ES2 plug-in. Start with all oscillators set to sawtooth waves. Use three oscillators in unison with the first lowest, the second one octave higher, and the third two octaves higher than oscillator one. If you only have two oscillators, you can get away with them tuned two octaves apart. Detune 12 cents up for oscillator two, and 12 cents down for oscillator three for a realistic, slightly-off Moog effect. Set the filter cutoff low, and turn up the filter envelope to shape the filter. Attack should be around 50 ms, decay about nine seconds, sustain in the middle of its range, and release the same as the decay setting. Turn the resonance about halfway up for some wah. I used ES2's "fat" button on the filter, as well as the extra sine-wave oscillator to make things Moog beefy. Alternatively, you could use an EQ plug-in with the 100–400 Hz range goosed up. Now set the amplitude envelope with a short attack around 15 ms, no decay, sustain full up, and release around two seconds. Make sure the keyboard assign mode is set to mono, so that only one note sounds at a time.

Now let's move on to the chords. Don used the behemoth Yamaha CS-80 analog synth (and a whole lot of reverb) to lay down some pretty authentic cathedral organ sounds. Here I made use of Native Instruments' sweet Massive virtual analog soft synth, but most virtual analog synths will work, provided their oscillators feature pulse-width modulation.

We'll use two oscillators for this patch, both set to a pulse wave. Tune the second oscillator two octaves up from the first for high organ overtones. Set the initial pulse width knob halfway between square and super thin (i.e., where the sound thins to nothing). Now use the modulation routing section (also known as the mod matrix) to route an LFO to affect pulse width. Set the LFO to a triangle wave at about 3 Hz. Be careful not to set the mod depth so deep that the wave peters out at the extremes; this is easier to dial in if you solo each oscillator when setting modulation. The filter cutoff is wide open; I bypassed Massive's entire filter section. Set the amplitude envelope for a quick attack (around 20 ms), no decay, full sustain, and just enough release so it doesn't sound like an on/off switch. You'll want to add a subtle chorusing effect, either on the synth itself or with another plug-in. I also added an EQ bump around 400 Hz for warmth. Finally, set up a really big stereo reverb (something with "church" or "cathedral" in the patch name is good!) using a send to an aux bus in your mixer window, and feed both the Moog bass and the organ sound to it. By the way, the "swoop" effects are really just the organ sound having its pitch swept dramatically with the Yamaha CS-80's large ribbon controller, so if you have a ribbon, route this to a wide pitch range and go to town. If you don't have a ribbon, you could easily substitute a pitch wheel, joystick, or even a knob with a wide pitch range.

The choir sounds were created with Roland VP330 Vocoder/String ensemble, which has its own unique nasal tone to make it a little tough to reproduce. Some nice choir "ahh" samples are probably the easiest solution.

You can download my Moog bass patch for Apple Logic ES2, as well as my organ patch for Native Instruments' Massive, sounds samples, and some suggestions on how to play "Mr. Crowley" at www.keyboardmag.com or at www.celebutantemusic/keybmag. Thanks for reading, and don't let me catch you eyeing any of them bats. . . .

Here's my Native Instruments Massive organ patch. You can quickly route the LFO to modulate pulse width by dragging LFO five over to the squares underneath the "Pulse Width" knobs in the oscillator section.

JAPANESE DANCING

How to Make Richard Barbieri's Pulsating Arpeggios

FEBRUARY 2008

Japan is one of those unique bands that never made a big splash in the U.S., but managed to be big stars just about everywhere else. Beginning as a brash glam rock outfit, they evolved during the early '80s to become moody and sophisticated new romantic art-rockers, unquestionably the missing link between early Roxy Music and Duran Duran. Making use of Roland modular synths, as well as the de rigueur Prophet-5 and Oberheim OB-X polysynths, keyboardist Richard Barbieri is a master of dark washes and subtly engaging sequences.

I had a hard time choosing a Japan track this month. There are plenty of gorgeous classic analog tones on their seminal 1980 release, *Gentlemen Take Polaroids* (made even more quaint by today's obsolescence of Polaroid cameras!). Since playable arpeggio parts are always fun and musically useful, this month we'll break down the arpeggio figure that introduces and plays throughout Japan's "Methods of Dance." When I say "playable," I'm referring to an arpeggio figure that starts and stops as well as transposes when playing the keyboard, as opposed to an arpeggio that latches "on" and plays in the same key regardless of notes played on the keyboard . . . boring!

On the original recording, Richard made use of a vintage Roland System 700 modular synth "played" by an Oberheim analog sequencer, but we'll make our lives easier by using modern plug-in synths. I used Arturia's Jupiter-8V virtual synth. I mainly chose it to utilize its vintage-style pattern sequencer, but there are numerous other plug-ins containing built-in sequencers, such as Native Instruments Massive, Arturia's 2600V and Moog Modular V, and Way Out Ware's KikAxxe.

First, let's set up the basic patch; this is pretty straightforward. Select sawtooth waveforms on both oscillators, and set them to the same octave. I used the 16' setting. You'll want to detune the oscillators against each other a bit for a nice chorusing effect. Set the oscillator volumes to the same level in the mixer section. Filter cutoff should be right near the middle of its range; we don't want to hear a lot of the saw waves' "teeth." Crank the resonance up to about 75 percent. Since this sound is very analog, effected, and murky, we're shooting for very mid-rangey timbre. I also used the Jupiter-8V's high-pass filter to remove low frequencies. If you don't have a high-pass filter, you can always use your DAW's EQ to knock the low end off.

This patch doesn't use the filter envelope, so set it to zero. Moving on to the amplitude envelope, set attack to zero, decay for a quick percussive envelope, say 300 ms, and sustain and release to zero.

Now for the fun part. First, set the sequence length to eight steps (use the sliding bar at the top of the grid on the Jupiter-8V). Now route the step sequencer to control the pitch of the oscillators. There are pop-up destination menus in the sequencer section, where I selected VCO1 and VCO2 on the Jupiter-8V; this allows the sequencer to control pitch. In order for the pitch to track right, you'll need to turn the VCO output amount knobs up to .0484. I routed the third sequencer out to VCA and turned on the "retrigger" button. This allows the sequencer to trigger the amplitude envelope at every sequence step so it automatically plays perfect sixteenth notes. E-zee. Here's the eight-note sequence pattern, expressed in half-step intervals:

| 0 | + 5 | + 7 | 0 | 0 | + 5 | 0 | + 5 |

One quirk of the Jupiter-8V is that the steps set to zero all need to be set to 0.010, or else the rest of the notes will be a little off key; bug alert!

Now all you need to do is hold down A♭, E, and D♭ and you're there.

The finishing touches on this patch relate to adding the aforementioned analog "murk." I inserted a distortion effect after the VCO on the Jupiter-8V, a slow chorus/flanger, and a subtle sixteenth-note delay, locked to tempo (by the way, "Methods of Dance" is around 124 bpm). Though I used the Jupiter-8V's onboard effects, there's no reason you couldn't make use of your DAW's effects. This sound really invites a lot of experimentation; I found some neat effects by playing with the VCO pitch amount settings in the sequencers for odd harmonies, as well as by holding down different combinations of keys. I bet Richard didn't have this option back in 1980!

You can download the Jupiter-8V patch, as well as some audio sounds samples, at www.keyboardmag.com, or at www.celebutantemusic/keybmag.

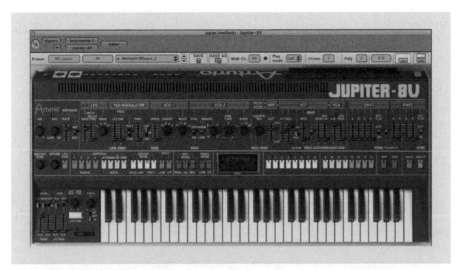

You can access the Jupiter-8V's step sequencer by clicking the button in the top right corner.

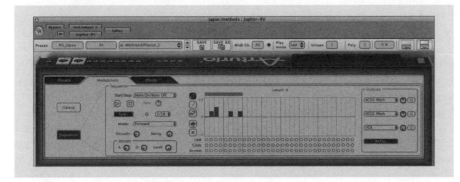

Click the modulation tab and the sequencer button and get your step sequence on!

BLOOP BLOOP, HEY, BLEEP BLEEP

Emulating Video Game Sounds

MARCH 2008

If you follow the electronic music underground, you may have noticed an odd little subgenre of electronic artists who use classic computer and game-console-type sounds, making for an intentionally lo-fi beep-fest. Styles range from the hardcore "chiptune" composers, who create instrumental music for imaginary video games, to the (slightly) more synth-pop leanings of artists such as 8-Bit Weapon and Freezepop. If you're motivated, there are a number of ways to use real vintage hardware to create the classic blips. On the low end, there's the inexpensive Synthcart cartridge for Atari 2600 game consoles, which is controlled by Atari's keypad controllers (qotile.net/synth.html). And for the serious bleep-ophobe, Elektron's SidStation is a standalone MIDI module using the same three-voice sound chip used in the Commodore 64 home computer from the eighties (www.sidstation.com).

But maybe you're not that hardcore. Maybe you have a modern computer with modern virtual synth plug-ins. Great, because we can use standard analog synth plugs to emulate old-school video games! The most important thing to remember about the old-school video game sound is the limitations, not only in the sounds themselves but in musical arrangement. Depending on the hardware, video games usually had severely limited polyphony, in many cases just two or three voices. And the tones themselves were often limited to easy-to-generate-in-digital square waves and noise. Given these limitations, the original "chiptune" composers frequently used tricks to add perceived complexity to their music and sound effects. We'll cover some of those too. Let's set up the basic patch, then I'll show some of these tricks.

Fire up a virtual analog synth and set one oscillator to a square wave. That's it for our oscillator. Moving on to the filter, set it to "band pass" if available. Set it somewhere in the middle of its range; we're just using it to generally lop off lows and highs and get rid of some of that darn fidelity. If you don't have a band-pass filter, you can use an EQ plug-in and just lop off lots of lows and highs. Make sure there's no filter envelope affecting the sound, and then set the amplitude envelope to a simple organ-type on/off shape. Attack and decay should be zero, sustain full up, and release on zero (you can tweak the attack and release up if you hear clicking).

All done, right? Wrong. It doesn't sound bad enough yet! Remember that 8-bit sound is a pretty unpure thing, and since most modern systems run at 24 bits, that's about 16 bits too many! In your DAW's channel strip, load up a bit-reduction plug (or "bitcrusher," as they're known) and go to town. I set Logic Pro's Bit-crusher to 8-bit resolution, and while I was at it, I set the downsampling to 4x, though you can mangle to your own taste. Just keep in mind that we want to sound like a video game, but not a Skinny Puppy video game.

And now for the tricks . . . one you've heard a zillion times in video games is the rapid ascending or descending glissando. These are super easy to make; just take that square wave and play a descending or ascending scale over five octaves into your sequencer, quantize it so it's perfectly even-sounding, and speed 'er up. Here's another trick: modulate the pitch of the oscillator with a fast-running LFO set to a square wave, with depth at exactly one octave. Another common old-school video game trick is the superfast arpeggio. Just play simple single-note triadic arpeggios, quantize them, and speed them way the heck up.

One more video game trick—try substituting the square wave with white noise. It's a good idea to route the keyboard tracking to filter cutoff, so high notes will be brighter than low ones, allowing you to play some crude beats. And for real madness, try automating the bitcrusher controls: instant Defender and Missile Command! Yee hah!

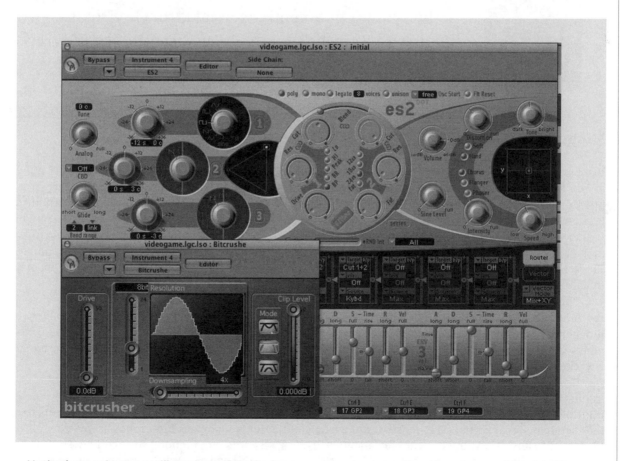

Notice how only one oscillator is used. In the lower corner, you can see how I made use of Logic's Bit-crusher to make our square wave sound authentically old-school.

REPLICATING REPLICANTS

Vangelis's Classic Blade Runner Pads

It comes as no surprise that Ridley Scott's 1982 dystopian sci-fi classic, *Blade Runner*, is a favorite among the synth cognoscenti. Its breakthrough visuals combined with Vangelis's forebodingly beautiful sound track have made it an enduring classic, and a "final cut" five-DVD boxed-set edition was released last year. And for us synth nuts, a three-CD sound track set was released as well, featuring all of Vangelis's music from the film as well as plenty of extra material.

Vangelis played a number of synths, but he's best known for his masterful use of Yamaha's CS-80 polysynth. Released in 1977, this 220-pound brute sounded great but fell short in patch storage and portability compared to its competition. Regardless, it sounded beautiful and was an incredible performance instrument; it was the first polysynth to feature weighted keys that sensed velocity and aftertouch. It also featured a huge pitch ribbon and a performance-friendly ring modulator. All this combined to make a formidable live performance synth, and Vangelis was perhaps the CS-80's greatest proponent. There are some great videos on YouTube of Vangelis demoing the CS-80 if you'd like to see the master in action.

This month we'll dig into Vangelis's famous swirling brassy pad textures with Arturia's CS-80V virtual reproduction of the Yamaha. Though the CS-80 has a rather unique voicing architecture (it's basically two independent eight-voice single-oscillator synths in one very heavy box!), you can still get the Vangelis vibe with a more standard polysynth; you can check out my CS-80-style Logic ES2 patch and audio at www.keyboardmag.com or www.celebutantemusic.com/keybmag.

If you already own Arturia's CS-80V, then you'll be familiar with its unique and occasionally confounding user interface (don't blame Arturia, it's just like the real thing). Unlike standard polysynths where multiple oscillators mix down into a single filter and voltage-controlled amplifier, the CS-80 contains two independent signal paths, each consisting of a single oscillator, a high-pass filter followed by a low-pass filter, and finally to a voltage-controlled amplifier. The two "synths" are then mixed together. This offers a lot of sonic shaping potential, but it's a little tricky to get your head around. Though the *Blade Runner* patch sounds very complex, it's simpler than it appears. First, set both oscillators to sawtooth waves in the same octave, and detune them by a tiny amount; it should not sound like chorusing. It'll sound a bit like a horn instrument when it's right.

Moving on to the filter, the original CS-80 contained 12-dB-per-octave filters, not the more common Moog/Prophet 24-dB slope. Without getting too techy, 12-dB filters are a bit brighter and buzzier, and this is important to the CS-80 character, so be sure to select this if you can. I used a mellow fixed frequency of 620 Hz for filter one with no resonance, and a very mellow filter sweep for filter two with attack at 800 ms and decay at 3000 ms. These times aren't critical, just keep 'em slow. I turned up the resonance about halfway to give it some "honk." If you're not using CS-80V, use the settings for the second filter I just described, and set the envelope sustain around 75 percent. Again, it should sound rather like a mellow horn. Amplitude envelope settings are much like the filter, slow 800-ms attack, full sustain, and longish 800-ms release.

Here's where we start getting tricky. The original CS-80 featured a built-in chorus effect, so turn it on (or use a plug-in) and make it pretty wet. A medium delay of around 300 ms is a good idea as well. Now our patch should be good and spacious. The other important ingredient of Vangelis's magic was his use of the CS-80's live performance controls, primarily its polyphonic aftertouch routed to control filter cutoff for swells, as well as vibrato. Poly aftertouch allows separate controller messages for each key, putting a lot of expressiveness under your fingertips, and the CS-80 was the first synth to feature it. Unfortunately, even now, there are very few controllers and synths that transmit polyphonic aftertouch, so you'll probably need to stick with mono aftertouch. Either way, configuring aftertouch to control the filter cutoff and vibrato amount will add a lot. Be careful, though, as a little aftertouch goes a long way. Set the control ranges for very subtle tonal shading and be wary of them replicants!

Arturia's CS-80V features two completely independent one-oscillator synths; you can see the two identical sets of controls across the middle. Oh yeah, and virtual cooling fans.

ORCHESTRAL MICRO-PRESETS IN THE DARK

OMD's Classic "Enola Gay" Lead Synth

MAY 2008

Formed in 1978, synth duo Orchestral Manoeuvres in the Dark were one of the U.K.'s earliest electro-pop bands. Influenced by electronic music innovators Kraftwerk and Brian Eno, they were part of the "first wave" of English electronic pop. Though their biggest hits on this side of the Atlantic were the digitally polished pop gems "If You Leave" and "So in Love" from the late '80s, their early U.K. hits "Electricity," "Maid of Orleans," and "Enola Gay" really put the old-school analog synths right out front. OMD was particularly fond of the Korg Micro-Preset M-500, and used it almost exclusively for lead lines in their early days. Originally released in 1977, this was an odd little single monosynth with 30 preset sounds that didn't sound too much like the instruments they were named for. But the Micro-Preset was cheap and cheery, and it cut right through a mix.

This month we'll cover the synth lead sounds used in OMD's hit "Enola Gay." If any of you own the classic tiny Casio VL-Tone keyboard, it's very similar to the "Fantasy" preset that's been used on numerous pop records. I used Arturia's Prophet-V, but you can create this patch on just about any two-oscillator synth. Begin by setting oscillator one to an 8' square wave (relatively high if your soft synth doesn't display octaves with footage). Now set oscillator two to a triangle wave one octave above . . . the often ignored triangle wave is our "secret sauce" in this patch. Since triangle waves have far fewer harmonics than the more common square and sawtooth shapes, they have less energy and therefore less volume. Here we want the high triangle wave to be louder than the sawtooth, so adjust oscillator one's volume considerably lower than oscillator two. Detune the two oscillators just a little to achieve a slight chorusing effect.

Now add some vibrato by routing a low-frequency oscillator set to a triangle wave to modulate the pitch of oscillator two only. Speed should be rapid, about 5 Hz, and depth should be about one-quarter step either way. The filter cutoff knob should be wide open. You can thin out the sound by turning up the resonance knob. The thinner we get, the more our Korg starts sounding like a Casio! Filter envelope will be set to zero, so it has no effect on the cutoff frequency. Finally, the amplitude envelope will be a simple "on/off" type affair; attack at zero, decay at zero, sustain full up, and just a tiny bit of release time (about 100 ms).

Orchestral Manoeuvres in the Dark managed to get more mileage from their mere Micro-Preset using clever doubling and panning of similar parts. They also changed up the sounds a bit. If you pan the original track hard left, you can hear the first synth line is a single-oscillator lower-register patch. You can imitate this patch by disabling oscillator one, and playing the oscillator triangle wave patch with vibrato one octave lower than normal. Adding some outboard chorusing and reverb to these patches really helps liven them up as well. Don't be afraid to get creative with panning. I like to pan a synth sound to the left, use an effects send to route it to a bus with a chorus effect inserted, then pan the chorus bus to the right. Going further with this concept, you can use a slightly different version of the patch from the one above—pan it to the right, then route it to another effects bus with a chorus or delay, and pan the effects bus to the right. It's easy to see where things can get pretty wide, pretty fast. All of those pans really let you dial in the stereo effect much more accurately then a standard preset stereo synth sound, and you'll be able to adjust the volumes of the different elements to make room for other things (like pesky singers!).

Most soft synths have preset modulation busses, but with Arturia's Prophet-V, you'll need to push up the mod wheel to get the LFO going . . . just like a real Prophet-5!

WICKI-DUKA-WICKI-DUKA-BOOM-BOOM!

Re-Create Herbie Hancock's Funky "Rockit" Lead

JUNE 2008

Herbie Hancock is a tremendous innovator, and one of his many career milestones is the electro-funk jam "Rockit." If you had MTV in 1983, this track was unavoidable, not only for its infectious vocoder-infused funk groove, but also for its bizarre (and slightly creepy) video clip, featuring hacked-apart dancing animatronic mannequins. It's hard to explain in print, but the effect was part kitschy, part funky, and certainly a bit unsettling. Herbie's groovin' synths and rapid-fire machine-gun drumbeats made the perfect foil for the video. In a typically '80s video maneuver, we see Herbie rockin' the lead on an E-mu Emulator I sampler, but the sound more likely emanated from an analog polysynth, and that's why we're here. This month we'll re-create the sweet synth lead from "Rockit." You'll need to provide your own funkiness, though!

If you listen close, you can hear each note has a little timbral movement in it; it's not a static waveform. This movement can be achieved using pulse-width modulation, or PWM. What the heck does this mean? An analog oscillator (or its virtual equivalent) can create fat, hollow-sounding square waves or thin, reedy-sounding pulse waves. PWM allows the width of the waveform to be modulated by either a low-frequency oscillator (for constant movement), or by an envelope generator (for a "one-shot" timbral change). It's a great way to animate static sounds, and in addition to offering timbral change, PWM tends to add a moderate chorus-like, pitch-change effect. Let's apply this idea to our "Rockit" lead, shall we?

I used a Native Instruments Massive virtual synth. True to its moniker, it offers a tremendous variety of virtual analog goodies, but you should be able to create this month's patch on just about any virtual analog synth that allows waveform pulse width to be modulated by an envelope generator. We'll start with two oscillators and detune them by a tiny amount for a doubling effect. Set the waveforms of each to "PWM" and dial the pulse-width controls into a pure square wave. This should be the thickest-sounding position of the pulse-width control. Now route an ADSR envelope generator to control pulse width. This is set on most synths in the modulation matrix, which is just a groovy name for "place where you route modulation sources to modulation destinations." In the case of Massive, you simply drag "1 Env" over to one of the boxes directly beneath the parameter you wish to modulate, then drag the mouse arrow over the box to increase the mod level. Make sure to repeat this for both oscillators. You'll want to set the mod envelope's attack to zero, and the decay to around 400 ms. Play with the mod amount until you hear the wave go from full and fat to so thin it almost disappears. Now we have timbral animation "built in" to the patch. I skipped the filter section altogether in this patch, but you can dial back the cutoff control if it's too bright. The volume envelope should have a straight-ahead on/off–style shape: attack at zero, sustain full up, and release close to zero.

If you like, you can add another oscillator one octave down, but judging from the video clip, it looks as if Herbie just doubled the riff in octaves with both hands. Finally, I added a small slap reverb in Massive, as well as inserting a Logic Sample Delay set to 100 samples on the left and 300 samples on the right to stereo-ize the sound a bit. Now quit playing with those creepy mannequins and get programming!

Here's what the Native Instruments Massive patch for Herbie's "Rockit" lead sound looks like. Note the little blue outlines around the pulse-width knobs that indicate modulation amount. The big envelope graphic represents the modulation curve for oscillator pulse width.

DUEL OF THE
MOOG JESTER

Chick Corea's Wicked Minimoog Lead

This month we pay tribute to two giants of the keyboard world: Chick Corea and the world's most revered monosynth, the mighty Minimoog. We're gonna rewind the way-back clock to 1976, when the bell-bottoms were big and the Pintos were flammable. Along with the Mahavishnu Orchestra, Chick's Return to Forever was at the cutting edge of the new fusion sound, combining the harmonic complexity of jazz with the power of electric instruments. Chick made a name for himself as one of the biggest proponents of the Rhodes electric piano, but he also played a mean Minimoog. Keep in mind that synths were still brand-new in the public eye; the Mini had only been released five years earlier, in 1971.

Return to Forever's final disc, 1976's *Romantic Warrior*, features virtuoso performances and some pretty wild Mini solos. Luckily for those of us who can't afford a vintage Minimoog, there are some sweet virtual Minis out there. There's Arturia's Minimoog V, as well as GForce's awesome Minimonsta, which I used for this month's installment. Of course there's always Moog's Little Phatty and Minimoog Voyager for those who just gotta have some genuine Moog analog phat-itude. Whichever you choose, turn it up, because we're going to re-create Chick's lead Mini sound from the classic Return to Forever track "Duel of the Jester and the Tyrant."

Let's start at the top with our oscillators. The Mini had three different square and pulse wave options, each with its own pulse width. The square wave is the widest and fittingly delivers the thickest tone, while narrower pulse width gives a thinner sound. For this patch, we're going to use the "in-between" pulse wave setting for oscillators one and two. Oscillator three won't be used as a sound generator, but instead as a modulation source; more on this later. (See figure 1 for the settings.) Now for the really important part of nailing Chick's tone: oscillator two's fine-tune setting is really crucial. If you're using a real analog synth, just tune as close as you can to oscillator one. We don't want it detuned like a chorusing effect; we want to hear a tight, almost flanger-like tone as the oscillators almost lock. Some soft synths (like Minimonsta) will accurately reproduce this "imperfection" when tuned exactly together, but most will lock together with digital perfection, which is not what we're going for. In this case, detune the second oscillator just a tiny bit.

Now that we have our oscillator magic, we'll set up our filter for just a little bit of plucky attack; see figure 3. That's almost everything. The only other missing ingredients are the pitch and mod wheels that Chick was goin' crazy with! You can set the pitch bend range to taste (a whole step usually works well). What about that mod wheel? Remember how we mentioned that oscillator three would be used as a mod source? These days, most synths feature dedicated low-frequency oscillators. LFOs generally run at frequencies below audible range, and they're not used as sound sources. Instead, they can be used to modulate pitch, filters, or amps for vibrato, wah, tremolo, and a slew of other neat effects. The original Minimoog didn't have a dedicated LFO. Instead, it allowed oscillator three to be switched from a standard tone source to a "lo" mode, where it could then be routed to control the aforementioned destinations. See figure 2 for the settings. Chick's Minimoog patch is now yours to jam out with. Be careful not to leave that Mini in the back of the Pinto on a hot day!

Fig. 1. To nail Chick with the oscillators. Tune oscillator one and two to the same 4' register. Then set the tuning of oscillator two to match oscillator one, but not quite.

Fig. 2. To get Chick's awesome vibrato, set oscillator three to LO mode, and turn on the Oscillator Modulation switch to route oscillator three to oscillators one and two.

Fig. 3. Set the filter cutoff low, around 25 percent open; we're going to let the filter envelope open it up for us. I set the resonance (emphasis in Moog-speak) at around 20 percent just to make things a little less hi-fi. Amount of Contour, aka filter envelope amount, is almost all the way up at around 80 percent. Filter envelope attack is zero, decay at one second, and sustain level almost full up. Loudness Contour, aka volume envelope, is set to a simple on/off shape. Attack is zero, decay 600 ms, and sustain all the way up.

THIS SYNTH'S FOR HIRE

Re-Create Springsteen's "Dancing in the Dark" Synth Pads

The keyboard community lost a tremendous talent in April of 2008 with the sad passing of longtime E Street Band keyboardist Danny Federici. He was best known for his tasteful organ chops in classic Springsteen anthems like "Rosalita" and "Born to Run." His partner in crime, Roy Bittan, contributed some great synth work to "I'm on Fire," "Glory Days," and "Dancing in the Dark," all from Springsteen's smash comeback, *Born in the U.S.A.* Roy's understated synth tracks emanated from just two keyboards: a Yamaha CS-80 for warm analog textures, and a Yamaha DX7 for bright, percussive digital timbres. This month we'll demonstrate how to create the mellow brass pads Roy used for the signature synth riffs of "Dancing in the Dark."

This month I'll use Native Instruments' Massive virtual analog plug-in, but you can use just about any two-oscillator soft or hardware synth. If the filter on your synth has a 12-dB-per-octave setting, use it. This is the type used by the Yamaha CS-80, so we can get a little more realistic re-creation. More filter mumbo-jumbo to come . . .

Start by setting two oscillators to sawtooth waves. Massive has a couple of different saws to choose from. I went with the warmest, smoothest ones (called "Sqr-Saw II," as Massive oscillator waves have the unique ability to morph to other shapes, but we won't be using that here). The oscillators are tuned down an octave to set the correct range, but they're both tuned to the same register. I then detuned oscillator two by 0.12 cents for a chorusing effect. Using Massive's drag-and-drop modulation routing, I moved "5 LFO" and "6 LFO" to oscillators one and two, respectively, to add a miniscule amount of vibrato to each. This is a really subtle thing; if your synth only has one LFO, you can use the same one for both oscillators. I did this to approximate the small amount of oscillator drift in a real analog synth.

I then set the filter for a 12-dB-per-octave (aka two-pole) slope, just like a CS-80. A 12-dB-per-octave filter's cutoff slope is less steep than the more common 24-dB-per-octave slope, allowing more frequencies through near the cutoff frequency. The result is a brighter tonality. Resonance should be set to zero. You'll want to turn up the filter envelope amount a bit and create an envelope with a medium fast attack, slow decay, medium sustain level, and just a bit of release. You may need to experiment to get the cutoff and envelope settings just right; we want our patch to be round and mellow like a French horn (check out my audio examples online to help with this).

Moving on to the amplitude envelope, tweak this so it's very similar to the filter envelope: medium quick attack, slow decay, medium sustain level, and a little bit of release. Once everything's dialed in, you'll want to add effects. The Yamaha CS-80 had a built-in chorus effect, and it seems most players left it permanently in the on position. Massive has a nice built-in chorus effect, so I used it. I also added a tiny smidge of built-in reverb from its second effects generator. If your virtual analog doesn't have built-in effects, you can use plug-ins in your DAW environment.

Here's Native Instruments' Massive, set up for the "Dancing in the Dark" pad. Note the little numbers in the oscillator, filter, and amp sections that represent the soft synth's drag-and-drop modulation routings.

ELECTRIC PIANO DREAMS COME TRUE

Faux Clav, Hall and Oates Style

I was recently called upon to learn the bouncy Hall and Oates gem "You Make My Dreams." Straight from the top, this is a tune made for keyboard players. But even after listening with my "let's nail the sound" ears, for some reason it didn't click right away. There I was, using the Logic EVD6 Clavinet virtual instrument, some overdrive and lo-fi plug-ins, and a gaggle of EQ, shaking my head going, "nope, nope, nope." How tough could this be? This is what I do, right? That's when I had my "Eureka!" moment. I vaguely recalled seeing a large and wooden keyboard bearing the Yamaha logo in the video I might have seen ages ago. Here's the silly part: I just sold my large and wooden Yamaha CP-30 electric piano a couple months back. Why didn't I instantly recognize the sound of a keyboard I just owned? Old age, I guess, and I don't mean the instrument.

So what's a Yamaha CP-30? That'd be a very substantial late-'70s vintage electronic piano used by the likes of Hall and Oates, Fleetwood Mac, Greg Hawkes of the Cars, and Gary Numan. It's all electronic, and as far as I can tell, used a divide-down oscillator scheme enabling full-keyboard polyphony. Sort of like an organ, but with more piano-like envelopes, and two full sets of oscillators for nice chorusing and doubling effects. And built like a brick . . . er, tank. Depending on the settings, it can go from mellow quasi-Rhodes, to bright clav/harpsichord-like tones. It didn't take long before I figured out how to nail the sound of the CP-30 using virtual synths, so the pre-MIDI behemoth's days in my studio were numbered.

Let's start makin' dreams come true! Start up any poly virtual analog-synth plug-in with two oscillators—I used Apple Logic Pro's ES2. If your synth's oscillators have a pulse wave with a variable pulse width setting, use it, and dial the width almost as narrow as it goes. If you make it too thin, the sound disappears, so be careful. If your synth doesn't have a pulse width setting, just choose the skinniest pulse wave option. Now set oscillator two to the same range, and set it to a thin pulse wave as well. If you can, make it a little wider for extra tone color. Detune the oscillators from each other for some natural chorus effect; I set one up seven cents and the other down seven cents. Moving on to the filter, use a 12-dB-per-octave filter if available (that's what most Yamaha keyboards had in those days), and set the cutoff low, resonance to zero. We'll use the filter envelope to make a plucky envelope. Turn up the envelope amount parameter, set the filter envelope attack to zero, the decay to about 5000 ms, sustain level to zero, and release to 50 ms. Keep in mind that even at its pluckiest, the CP-30 isn't very bright, so don't be tempted to open the filter up too much. You can hear this pretty clearly on the opening of the Hall and Oates track (and be sure to listen to our online examples too). The amplitude envelope should be set similarly to the filter envelope, except for decay, which should be around 1000 ms.

We're close, but our sound is way too "hi-def" to be right. First, I dialed in just a touch of ES2's built-in distortion and chorusing. Now it was getting there, but still too hi-fi for the '70s, so I inserted an EQ plug-in after the synth and did some major carving. I knocked off 17 dB with a low-shelf EQ set at 184 Hz, boosted 5 dB at 600 Hz, and boosted 6.5 dB at 3150 Hz with a high-shelf EQ. This removed the thick bass, goosed the mids, and brought back a little definition up top. Now it had the funky mid-range honk of a real Yamaha CP-30!

I've created audio samples to help you dial this guy in. You can check them out at www.keyboardmag.com or www.celebutantemusic.com/keybmag. You can also download my "You Make My Dreams" patch for use with the ES2 synth plug-in in Apple Logic Pro.

Want an '80s lo-fi sound from a high-voltage soft synth? No problem. Start with any two-oscillator synth, such as Apple Logic ES2.

CLONE THE DOCTOR WHO SOUND

Originally airing in 1963, *Doctor Who* featured some pretty far-out electronic music and sound effects courtesy of the BBC Radiophonic Workshop. *Doctor Who*'s original run predated modern voltage-controlled analog synthesizers; its music and effects were improvised from a primitive collection of test oscillators and some very creative use of found sound and music concrète–style tape-looping techniques. The theme was composed by Ron Grainer, but it was painstakingly created and spliced together by the little-known pioneer Delia Derbyshire, one of the first female electronic musicians.

You can easily make *Doctor Who*'s signature synth lead on any virtual analog soft synth or hardware synth; in fact, it's the perfect sound to try to emulate when you're learning your way around a synthesizer. Just choose one that has a sine wave as a waveform option on at least two oscillators. I used Way Out Ware's TimewARP 2600, a nifty virtual analog reproduction of the classic ARP 2600 semi-modular synthesizer.

1. Start with a sine wave on oscillator one. This gives you almost the entire lead sound.
2. There's a slightly more "twinkly" sound subtly layered in with the lead; I achieved this by using the 2600's ring modulator. A ring modulator sums two signals together, but only outputs the "difference" frequencies. This often results in all manner of sideband noise madness, but here I'm just combining oscillators one and two and mixing it in a tiny bit. I did this by taking oscillator one's saw out and routing it to one of the ring mod ins, and the setting oscillator two to "low"-frequency LFO mode and routing it to ring mod input two. If your synth doesn't have ring mod, you could achieve a similar effect by setting oscillator two an octave up from the first one, and using a bit of LFO tremolo (or even vibrato) on it. The secret is that the second oscillator needs to stay very quiet in the mix.
3. Add lots of portamento (also known as "glide") to re-create the *Doctor Who* swooping sound. You can experiment with the time; on TimewARP 2600, I found 0.164 seconds worked well.
4. Don't use any filter envelope at all, and set the amplitude envelope like a standard organ-type on/off shape. Use a medium attack so it doesn't click on, but zero decay, full sustain, and quick release.
5. Add plenty of good and cheesy spring reverb. I used TimewARP 2600's built-in "reverberator," turned all the way up.

Finally, I totally cheated and used Audio Damage's awesome Fluid chorus plug-in on the insert. For fun, I threw together a little mock arrangement of the Doctor Who theme. I created the bass line at the top by using a single-note electric guitar sample with Logic Audio's Pitch Shifter II plug doing duty as an octaver—warbly!

You can see where I routed oscillators one and two to TimewARP 2600's ring modulator on the left. You actually don't need to, as oscillators one's and two's connections are "normalized" to the ring mod section; I just added virtual cables to clarify the signal flow.

PROGRAM FUNKY SYNTH BASS

by Jason Miles

Here are some tips on how to program some really funky bass sounds. You can use these ideas to pull up great sounds on hardware synths like the vintage Minimoog, Moog Voyager, and Minimoog Old School, or on any number of software synths that work similarly.

Check out the programming details and screenshots from GForce Minimonsta to learn how to make two different types of killer synth bass sounds—one that's fat and round, the other that's sharp and biting. And remember, these are just the basics—it's up to you to tweak and get funky on your own. If you don't already know, once you start playing it, you'll discover that the Minimoog is one instrument for the ages.

BASS SOUND 1: SHARP AND BITING

Attack: Set at zero with the Attack Time knobs on both the Filter and Loudness Contour sections. It has to be to get that bite you want.

Decay Time and Sustain Levels: Set at 40 percent. This doesn't make the sound too fluffy, and still gives it enough sustain to bend and slide notes.

Frequencies: I want some bite, but I don't want to lose the bottom. My settings are 40 percent for the frequency (Cutoff Freq knob) and envelope modulation (Amount of Contour knob) to make the sound pop. I now add resonance with the Emphasis knob turned to about 60 percent.

Waveform: This choice is important since it defines the character of the tone. On this patch, I use a sawtooth on oscillator one (the top dial shown here) and a square wave on oscillators two and three. It gives the sound a solid punch, and the square wave makes the track sound full.

BASS SOUND 2: FAT AND ROUND

Waveform: I use square waves on all oscillators, as shown.

Tuning: I slightly detune oscillator two. It just widens the sound.

Decay and sustain: If you make the decay and sustain short, the sound will actually get smaller because it doesn't resonate over the track the same way. I make sure that my decay times are at about 40 percent and the sustain levels are at about 30 percent. This adds a good length to the note when you play it.

Attack Time: Down to 0.

Cutoff Freq: I set it to 40 percent.

Emphasis: Almost 50 percent.

Amount of Contour: Start with 30 percent and taper it down from there if you need to.

LET YOUR KICK DRUM SOUND GUIDE YOUR SYNTH BASS TONE

Though I get inspiration for bass lines in many ways, here's one method for figuring out what Minimoog bass sound to use: If you already have a drum groove, listen to the kick drum. If the kick has a big, fluffy sound, add more attack by turning down the Attack Time knob; with a sharper-sounding kick, lower the filter frequency using the Cutoff Freq knob and let that fill up the bottom of the track.

MAKE THE "FRANKENSTEIN" MONSTER LEAD SOUND

The Edgar Winter Group's classic space-rock jam "Frankenstein" may well be the super-grooviest tune ever committed to wax, thanks in no small part to Edgar's squirrely ARP 2600–powered lead synth. Edgar may have been one of the very first keytar players: he took the 2600's somewhat unwieldy four-octave keyboard controller, attached a strap, slung that sucker over his shoulder, and traded licks with guitarist Rick Derringer. He also worked the left-hand controls like a madman. There's a pretty neat live video on YouTube where Edgar gets down with the 2600's keyboard's pitch knob and also flips the resonance on and off. Not to mention that Edgar plays sax and a drum solo, all in the same song!

I'll be using Way Out Ware's TimewARP virtual 2600 plug-in to re-create the "Frankenstein" lead, but you could also use Arturia's 2600V, or just about any virtual analog synth with a ring modulator, which is the key to nailing this sound. What's a ring modulator, you say? It's an old-school electronic processor that combines two waveforms and outputs only the sum and difference frequencies of the waves. It's not too important to understand the theory, but the sound is usually pretty recognizable; ring mod tones are typically rich in odd harmonics, and sound pretty grindy. In this patch, the results aren't too nasty because we're tuning the two oscillators to a perfect fifth (less consonant intervals make for nastier overtones). Here's how to do it.

1. Set oscillator one to a saw wave. If you're using a 2600 clone, route a virtual patch cable from the sawtooth out jack to the VCO 1 input in the audio mixer section (see screenshot). This wave also goes to the left side-ring modulator input, but in a 2600, it automatically gets routed there unless you override

it with a virtual patch cord.

2. Set oscillator two to a square wave by setting the pulse width to 50 percent, and tune it up a perfect fifth from oscillator one. Plug the pulse wave out into the right side input of the ring modulator.

3. In the audio mixer section, turn the ring mod and oscillator one all the way up. Turn oscillator two down to zero (its pulse wave out should be going straight to the ring mod).

4. Set the filter cutoff frequency all the way open, and the resonance on zero.

5. If you're using a 2600 clone, set the amplitude envelope attack and release times to zero. For synths with standard ADSR-style envelopes, set attack, decay, and release to zero, and sustain to max.

6. For 2600 clones, turn up the VCF and AR faders to max in the VCA mixer section, as well as the VCA fader in the final mixer on the right. For other synths, you should be all set.

7. Sprinkle in a dash of portamento to make notes glide smoothly from pitch to pitch.

Edgar also does some deft filter cutoff and resonance manipulation in the synth solo sections. The best way to emulate this is to assign external faders or knobs to these controls. Don't forget to assign the mod wheel to LFO vibrato depth to add vibrato. And finally, make sure to grow out yer hair and strap that keyboard on. Happy re-animating!

Here's the "Frankenstein" lead sound, as rendered with Way Out Ware's TimewARP 2600 soft synth. Note that oscillator one's saw wave goes to the ring mod's left input, and oscillator two's pulse wave goes to the ring mod's right input, with both inputs at equal volume.

JOE WALSH'S "LIFE'S BEEN GOOD" SYNTH RIFF

JANUARY 2009

Not only did Joe Walsh man the keys on some of the Eagles' best-known hits, but he's a bona fide synth and electronics nut. He's amassed an impressive collection of analog synths over the years, and he sneaks 'em into his solo work—notably his 1978 hit, "Life's Been Good."

Joe created the song's percolating synth riff on an ARP Odyssey and an analog sequencer. The neat part about this 16-note sequence is that the synth's oscillators repeat the same note; the "melody" is the sequencer controlling the filter cutoff frequency. This is because the filter resonance is dialed high enough to "self-oscillate," or ring, becoming a sound source independent of the oscillators. Instead of routing the sequencer's control voltage to the oscillators for pitch control, Joe routed it to the filter cutoff, "playing" the melody on the filter. The synth's oscillators just bonked away on A (the root note of the song), creating a two-voice effect from a monophonic synth.

To re-create this on a soft synth, we'll get the same effect from playing the keyboard that Joe did from a sequencer. We'll need a synth that can disconnect the keyboard from the oscillators while letting the keyboard control the filter cutoff. The latter is a no-brainer—most synth filters have a "keyboard tracking" setting that does just this. The tricky part is that not all synths let you disconnect the keyboard. Most Minimoog or Prophet-5 emulators do; it's called "osc 3 control" on a Mini, or just hit the "keyboard" button on oscillator two of a Prophet-5. You can also do this on a virtual modular (e.g., Arturia's Moog Modular V) by plugging the keyboard CV into the filter instead of the oscillators, just like Joe! From here, let's take it step by step.

1. Turn down all the oscillators except for the one that's not affected by the keyboard.
2. Set the "keyboard-less" oscillator to a sawtooth wave and tune it to a low A note.
3. Make sure the filter is in low-pass mode, preferably 24 dB per octave.
4. Turn the keyboard tracking all the way up and the resonance almost all the way up (on a soft Minimoog, turn on the "keyboard control" switches).
5. Make sure the volume is down, because the filter resonance can get loud.
6. You might have to experiment to make sure the keyboard is tracking correctly; check this by playing octaves.
7. Once the filter is tracking in octaves, fine-tune the cutoff frequency to the correct pitch by matching the pitch to the oscillator's A note.

8. Tweak the resonance until you hear the right mix of oscillator-to-filter ring.

9. Set the amplitude envelope for a quick attack, and dial the decay and release to a medium time.

Now play the riff shown in the image. Remember, the oscillator is playing A no matter what key you hit—hitting the correct notes moves the filter cutoff, creating the right pitch at each step. To match the record, I added a stereo doubler (around 25 ms) and a spring reverb simulator. Enjoy, and no wrecking hotel rooms!

Listen to audio examples at www.keyboardmag.com or www.celebutantemusic.com/keybmag. You can also download my "Life's Been Good" patch for GForce Minimonsta.

GForce Minimonsta, set up according to steps 1–9.

Notation for the "Life's Been Good" synth riff.

WHEN DOVES CRY, FINGERS FLY

FEBRUARY 2009

*B*oom kak-kak boom. Boom kak-kak boom. That just may be one of the most easily recognized song intros of all time. You gotta hand it to Prince. In addition to his utterly unique singing and songwriting, the guy has created his own sound palette at every stage of his career. Back in the *Purple Rain* era, his royal purpleness rocked out with an original LinnDrum drum machine (the aforementioned "kak kak" sound is a tuned-down Linn sidestick) and a pile of original Oberheim analog polysynths. This month we'll dig into the hyper-speed faux-violin solo that screams through the end of Prince's megahit "When Doves Cry."

For years I scratched my head trying to figure out how Prince managed such an impossibly fast and precise solo. Though there were hardware sequencers out by that time, judging by the cadence (and the 32nd-note grace notes), I'd be willing to bet it was played by hand with a half-speed tape machine. But it's still sort of fun to attempt it at full-tilt; I got pretty close, and I bet there's some of you out there with the chops to pull it off—Prince included. Either way, we're gonna whip up the cool faux-violin tone. You can make this sound on almost any virtual analog instrument; it doesn't take too much synth horsepower. For this month's example, I used Native Instruments Massive virtual instrument.

The sound uses just one oscillator. Instead of using the typical concept of detuning two oscillators for timbral depth, the "Doves" violin gets its mojo from using pulse-width modulation and some flanging to murk it up. Pulse-width modulation is a complicated way of saying that we're taking a plain ol' square wave and varying the width between a thin rectangle and a wide square, which gives the raw sound a lot more motion than a basic static waveform. Since it would be impractical to twirl the pulse-width knob back and forth all day long (unless you had a motivated intern), we'll use a low-frequency oscillator set to a triangle wave as a modulation source to do our knob twisting for us.

Begin by setting one oscillator to a pulse wave; it might say PWM. Set the pulse width in the middle, so that the raw wave is as big and thick as possible. Now we need to route a low-frequency oscillator (LFO) to control the pulse width. Some synths have a control for LFO amount near the oscillators; others will have it tucked away in a modulation matrix (see step 1). Set the LFO to a medium-speed sine or triangle wave (see step 2) and increase the intensity until the oscillator tone begins to peter out at its extremes; back it off to just before that happens. Our filter will be wide open for this patch, with no resonance. The amplitude envelope should have a pretty quick attack around 20–40 ms, but not zero; remember, this is supposed to sound like a violin going nuts. Decay should be pretty quick, and sustain almost zero. You'll be playing so fast that you shouldn't get that far! Release should be zero. Now you'll want to add some flanger effect either from the virtual synth or as an insert effect in your DAW. That's it! I'll see ya dancin' in the purple rain!

Step 1. See that little green number 5 under the Pulse Width knob? That's the LFO routed to modulate the oscillator pulse width. You can set the mod depth by holding down the Apple key and click/dragging on the number 5 on a Mac.

Step 2. Set your LFO to a triangle wave, medium speed, and then experiment with the intensity.

NINE INCH NAILS' "CLOSER" SYNTH BASS

Nine Inch Nails made their name bringing the harsh electro-dance sound of industrial rock to the masses. But in 1994 Trent Reznor slowed down the bpm and turned up the funk-o-meter with the slow burn of "Closer." The track sets the stage with a kick and snare sampled from Iggy Pop's underground classic "Nightclubbing," and fills out with a rezzy, slithering synth bass sure to be heard in "men's entertainment" establishments for decades to come. The track stacks elements as it goes, piling on machine-like synths and spooky backward pianos until the layers pile up into a throbbing monster, artfully concluding with a simple, eerie forward-backward piano melody line at the outro.

This month we'll re-create the "Closer" bass groove with a virtual instrument. Trent's never been specific about the source of the "Closer" bass tone, but a Minimoog has all the necessary sonic ingredients. We'll use Arturia's Minimoog V to re-create the burbling bassage, but most virtual analogs will get you close; try using a VA with fat-sounding filters!

1. Set two oscillators to sawtooth waveforms and set the pitch to 32' (that's real low for those without footage settings).
2. Detune one of the oscillators by about 10 percent.
3. Set the filter's cutoff frequency to almost zero and the resonance to about 60 percent (if you're a using a Moog emulator, it may be called "emphasis").
4. Turn the keyboard tracking all the way up so the cutoff frequencies open as you ascend the keyboard (on a Mini emulator, turn on both "keyboard control" switches next to the cutoff knob).
5. Set keyboard envelope level, or "amount of contour" up, to around 25 percent, then set the filter envelope attack to 400 ms, decay to 575 ms, sustain to 1, and release close to zero.
6. Amplitude envelope, or "loudness contour," should have attack at zero, decay at 250 ms, sustain full up, and release close to zero.

7. Make sure glide and legato are turned off if you're using a Minimoog emulator.

If you're using the Arturia Minimoog V, you're all set. If you're using anything else, here's where it gets a little tricky. The key to nailing the "Closer" bass patch is precise tweaking of the filter cutoff, resonance, and envelope amount settings—it may take a while to get them dialed in. I recommend listening to the original track, or better still, downloading my examples for quick comparisons. Then you can do what I do: Listen to just how bright the filter is, as well as how much "honk" the filter resonance setting is creating, and tweak accordingly. Finally, a touch of stereo chorus and some EQ will get you, uh, closer. I dropped out a little sub-bass at 70 Hz, and added a little lo-mid bump at 240 Hz to boost up the honk. Hope this helps bring the bass, NIN-style!

Whether you're using Arturia's Minimoog V (shown) or another virtual synth, be sure to tweak the filter cutoff, resonance, and envelope amount to get the "honk" of "Closer" just right.

THE ALAN PARSONS PROJECT'S "I ROBOT" BASS LINE

APRIL 2009

Alan Parsons's music is synonymous with the innovative sound palette and exacting production values that won him initial acclaim as recording engineer on Pink Floyd's *The Dark Side of the Moon*. The track "I Robot" was the climax of the Alan Parsons Project's 1977 album of the same name, and was a keyboard tour de force. It opens with layers of slowly phasing string machine and choral voices, making its way toward the signature sequenced synth bass line. That line has the same imposing, "robotic" quality as Pink Floyd's famous "On the Run" riff, but at a mellower, semi-funky '70s pace. In the '70s, most listeners' ears weren't accustomed to the perfectly timed feel of sequencers, so this was pretty cool stuff. We'll replicate it using the virtual analog section of Spectrasonics Omnisphere (reviewed Dec. '08), but it'll work great with any virtual analog synth.

1. Starting with an initialized patch, set an oscillator to a sawtooth wave. If using Omnisphere, make sure to click the synth button in the oscillator section, as this gives you virtual analog (as opposed to sample-based) mode. Set the octave low: –12 (or even –24) semitones, or 32' on synths that do it "pipe organ" style.

2. In the filter section, use a low-pass filter and set the cutoff frequency about 75 percent open, and resonance to zero.

3. Set the volume envelope attack and decay to zero, sustain full up, and release to zero.

4. Here's where we get the signature sound: Add a phaser. Nothing bright here—we want vintage MXR murk. I used Retrophaser from Omnisphere's built-in effects, with rate at 0.32 Hz, depth turned all the way up, and number of poles set to four.

5. Now we need a similarly murky tape delay. Logic has a great Tape Delay plug-in, but on something more general-purpose, you can get close by rolling off high frequencies, and most delay plug-ins let you

do this. The delay time on the original song sounds like it was about a half note, and given the song's tempo, around 630–640 ms worked for me.

6. Pan the synth hard left in your DAW's mixer, because we want dry synth on the left and delayed signal on the right. If your soft synth's built-in effects don't support this kind of panning, send the synth to an aux bus with the delay inserted (as I did in Logic), and   pan that bus hard right.

7. Finally, I inserted a Logic Channel EQ on the instrument channel, dialed out some sub-bass with a low shelf, and put a 5-dB bump at 270 Hz for added '70s low-mid warmth.

Now play or sequence the notes shown, and repeat. You, robot!

Omnisphere, set to synth mode with a sawtooth wave (step 1, below), low-pass filter (step 2), and straight on/off envelope (step 3).

DEPECHE MODE'S "POLICY OF TRUTH" LEAD LINE

MAY 2009

Depeche Mode always packs a double-fisted punch of hummable pop songs built on innovative synth programming. One technique they frequently employed was the deft blending of synths with samples of instruments, including orchestral brass, strings, choirs, and electric guitar. The intro and choruses of the hit "Policy of Truth," from their 1990 album *Violator*, are a great example. A harsh digital synth line seamlessly morphs into an overdriven slide guitar lick in a bit of auditory sleight of hand. We'll kick it old school and re-create the patch with Waldorf's PPG Wave 2.V plug-in. Though it's been around for some time, PPG Wave 2.V still sounds great and is available affordably in the Waldorf Edition package alongside Waldorf's D-Pole and Attack plug-ins [*note: Waldorf released an updated Wave 3.V virtual synth in 2010*]. You can also use any analog-style virtual instrument with "digital" waveforms, such as Logic's ES2, Korg's virtual M1 LE or Wavestation, or Arturia's Prophet VS.

To *really* make it sound like the record, create a sliding guitar sample for the tails of the final note in the signature synth line. It's a combination of a slide down from *G*, cross-faded into alternating B♭4 and G4 diads. Run those samples through a bitcrusher plug-in for that crusty eight-bit sampler effect you thought you'd never again use. That's what we swore—the time before. Hear audio examples at keyboardmag.com or celebutantemusic.com/keybmag. You can also download my "Policy of Truth" patch for Waldorf's PPG Wave 2.V soft synth.

1. Set up a basic patch by opening the filter cutoff all way up. Set the volume envelope to a basic "on/off" shape: attack and decay at zero, sustain full up, and a quick release.

2. The most important aspect of nailing this sound is getting the waveform right. The PPG Wave has 32 "wavetables," each containing 63 waveforms; these usually go from darkest to brightest in numerical order. Click the Digi button, then scroll the Wavetable selector to choose a wavetable.

3. Then click the Digi button again and select a wave with the Osc knob in the modifiers section. I used wave 57 from wavetable 23. If you're using another synth, compare the original song as well as my online examples to match the digital, harmonically rich timbre.

4. Once you've got something in the ballpark, dial the filter cutoff down so things aren't too "tingly," and add a tiny bit of resonance (Emphasis knob on the PPG). This will make our patch sound a little more organic.

5. The PPG also features a "sub-wave" function, which adds a second wave from the same wavetable. Using the Sub knob in the Modifiers section, I dialed in wave 58 for some extra harmonics an octave up.

6. Now add some chorus and reverb with external plug-ins. For high-quality chorus, I'm really digging Audio Damage's cheap and cheerful Fluid these days.

See where it says "OSC-WAVES-SUB"? That's where the magic happens on a PPG—these knobs cycle through a wavetable's 63 different waves.

MGMT'S "TIME TO PRETEND" SYNTH LEAD

JUNE 2009

New York duo MGMT has struck gold with their electro anthems "Time to Pretend" and "Kids," proving that a hooky melody always wins. Of course, a slick retro synth patch to play it on doesn't hurt. To cook up the "Time to Pretend" lead, we'll use Way Out Ware's TimewARP 2600, which faithfully emulates the classic ARP 2600 semi-modular analog synth. TimewARP 2600 is what the highly technical refer to as a "pretty honkin' synth"—it has tons of parameters and routing options. We'll use it in a straightforward way, though, so just about any virtual analog will work. The patch itself is only half the secret here—there are some key effects we'll bring in afterward.

Now we'll add some plug-in effects in the DAW. I used a subtle amount of Logic's Bitcrusher to make the tone a little more "in your face." Then I added EQ with a steep low-shelf roll-off from 440 Hz down, an 8-dB peak at 1300 Hz to emphasize the nasal honk, and a high shelf at 6500 Hz to dampen highs that'd make things sound too "hi-fi" otherwise. Finally, I added a medium amount of large, dark room reverb for sonic space—you can hear a similar one in the intro of the original MGMT track.

Go to keyboardmag.com/how-to or celebutantemusic.com/keybmag for this story with audio examples. You can also download the "Time to Pretend" patch for Way Out Ware's TimewARP 2600 soft synth.

1. This patch only uses one oscillator, set to a sawtooth wave. In TimewARP 2600, run a virtual patch cord from the "sawtooth" jack to the VCO 1 input in the VCF audio mixer section.

2. Using a low-pass filter (in four-pole or 24-dB-per-octave mode), set the cutoff about 75 percent open and resonance at 20 percent. The exact cutoff frequency on TimewARP 2600 is 2764 Hz.

3. Make the amplitude envelope a simple on/off type: attack, decay, and release at zero and sustain all the way up.

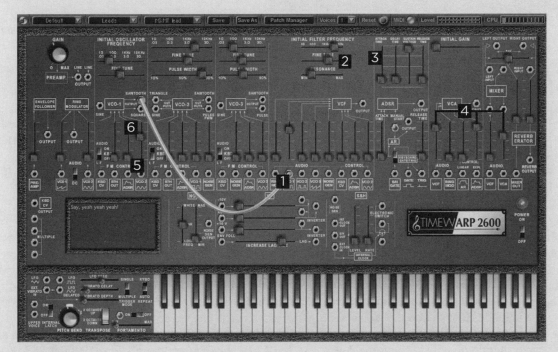

4. In TimewARP 2600's VCA mixer section, turn up the Audio VCF slider and Control ADSR slider, and finally, turn up the Audio VCA slider all the way at the right in the Mixer section.

5. Now we have a bland sawtooth patch. We spice it up by adding vibrato. Most synths call the relevant setting something like "LFO depth" or "pitch mod amount." In TimewARP 2600, any of the three oscillators can be switched to low-frequency (LF) mode, so I used oscillator 2 (VCO 2) to generate vibrato.

6. Then I turned up the VCO 2 slider (the one *in* the VCO 1 section) to modulate VCO 1's frequency. Use a sine or triangle wave set to about 7.3 Hz with depth set pretty deep.

The original ARP 2600 didn't have oscillator wave selector switches. Instead, each oscillator had a default waveform that you could override by plugging in patch cords. Here I've patched a sawtooth wave from VCO 1 into the filter's VCO 1 input.

THE STEVE MILLER BAND'S "FLY LIKE AN EAGLE"

Time keeps on slippin', slippin', slippin' into the future indeed. Released in 1976, Steve Miller's "Fly Like an Eagle" became an FM rock radio classic. But it also showed Steve's penchant for synth-driven space rock with the preamble to the "Fly Like an Eagle" track.

Like a lot of analog patches, this isn't too hard to replicate, and the secret is all in the fine-tuning. This month, I'll show you how to create the "Fly Like an Eagle" intro using GForce Minimonsta, a software Minimoog-and-then-some emulation, but almost any virtual analog synth set to monophonic mode will work.

Using either an aux send or an insert in your DAW software, add a delay, preferably one that can emulate the sound of vintage tape echo, i.e., with EQ to damp the highs for a murky sound. If you have a plug-in that purposely emulates tape delay, such as Line 6 Echo Farm or Logic's Tape Delay, so much the better.

Set the delay time to about 600 ms and feedback almost to the point of self-oscillation—around 50 percent works well. I set the high cut on my delay to 1900 Hz to keep it dark and murky. The delayed and dry signals should be equal in volume. I also inserted a low-shelf EQ, rolling off about 9 dB at 345 Hz, to remove some low-end ringing, but you may or may not need it.

Now break out those velvet posters and turn on the black lights. I initially thought a sequencer played the "Eagle" lines, but I was over-thinking the issue. All you need to do is steadily drag your finger up the white keys, starting on A and ending on E, two and a half octaves higher. Once you get the speed right, it'll sound exactly like the original intro. Listen to audio samples and download my "Fly Like an Eagle" patch for GMedia's Minimonsta at keyboardmag.com or celebutantemusic.com/keybmag.

1. Set both oscillators one and two to a medium-width pulse wave and tune to the same octave.

2. Detune oscillator two just a little.

3. Set oscillator one's mixer level at full volume and oscillator two's at about 25 percent.

4. Make sure the keyboard assign mode is set to mono and legato mode. This way you can simply drag your finger up the white keys to sound each note.

5. Make sure to disable the "glide" control to the left of the keyboard. (With it enabled, I was hearing too much note attack in Minimonsta.)

6. Set the filter cutoff to about 50 percent, resonance to zero, and envelope amount ("amount of contour" on a real or virtual Minimoog) to zero. You'll have to experiment with the cutoff as you listen to the song to get it just right.

7. Set the volume envelope ("loudness contour" in Moog-speak) to a simple, organ-like on/off shape: attack and decay at zero, sustain full up, and release at zero.

SEAL'S "CRAZY" COMP

AUGUST 2009

The pulsating synth chords of Seal's 1990 smash "Crazy" have made many synthesists exclaim, "How did they do that?" At first listen, it sounds like quantized sequencer work against a filter slowly opening and closing. On closer inspection, there's more going on. In re-creating this sound, instead of playing the syncopated chords as heard, I played them as sustained whole notes. I then gated those notes using a noise gate side-chained with a separate "trigger" synth. This nailed the choppier texture and rhythmic bounce of the original track.

Since we have a recorded sequence of sustained chords, this approach is more suited to recording than to covering "Crazy" in a live band. Listen to audio samples and download the Seal "Crazy" patch for Arturia's Jupiter-8V at keyboardmag.com/lessons or celebutantemusic.com/keybmag.

1. To create the main sound, I used Arturia's Jupiter-8V, but any virtual analog synth should work. Set both oscillators to thin pulse waves, with one oscillator an octave above the other. Detune them just enough for a nice chorusing effect.

2. Set the filter cutoff about halfway and the resonance all the way up. The Jupiter doesn't have a very screamy filter, so you may need less resonance on a different synth. We want the cutoff low enough that the filtered sound is organ-like but not whistley. Add some keyboard tracking (Key Follow in JP-8V) for more brightness as you ascend the keyboard. Set filter envelope amount at zero.

3. Modulate the filter cutoff with a slow triangle or sine LFO. You won't need much depth, just a subtle sweep.

4. Create a simple on/off volume envelope: attack, decay, and release at zero, and sustain full up.

5. Record this simple chord pattern into your sequencer at around 103 bpm. Hold each chord for a whole bar:

E5 | G5 | Asus4 | A5

6. Open a basic synth on another track. You won't actually hear this synth, so all that matters is that it has a straight on/off envelope to gate the main sound cleanly. Turn up send one on the trigger synth track. Set the send to pre-fader (done by option-clicking in Logic); this lets you turn down the fader so you don't hear the trigger synth without affecting the send output.

7. Exact routing will depend on your DAW, but in Logic, insert a noise gate on the main synth's channel (almost all DAWs have a similar gate plug-in), then make the gate's side-chain input listen to bus one. Play back the chord track, and "play" the "Crazy" rhythm with the trigger synth—you may need to adjust the gate's threshold to get it just right.

8. Finally, add a delay of around 294 ms to the Jupiter.

On the noise gate, make sure the reduction is all the way down for full muting between notes, and play with the threshold to get the gating just right.

THE "BILLIE JEAN" BASS SOUND

by Dave Polich

There are actually two bass lines for Michael Jackson's "Billie Jean"—the snaking main figure, and a secondary accent played a fifth above the root, falling only on the first and fourth eighth-notes of each bar. For the live version at the *This Is It* concerts, how was bassist Alex Al going to accomplish this? Two Minimoogs—that's how! You can replicate this using two instances of Arturia's Minimoog V, or nearly any virtual analog synth.

Alex dialed in the primary line, using a dark, rubbery bass sound, on his restored vintage Minimoog D, and played it with his right hand. To get this sound, set the first two oscillators to sawtooth waveforms, both at the 16' pitch. Filter cutoff is almost all the way down, filter emphasis (resonance) is just a bit up from minimum, and amount of contour (filter envelope amount on other synths) is set to 3. Set the filter envelope decay to about 210 ms and the sustain level to 8 to get a sound shape similar to an electric bass guitar. The decay switch is off, loudness contour (Moog-speak for volume envelope) decay time is at about two o'clock, and loudness sustain level is all the way up.

The accent line was a job for Alex's left hand on his Minimoog Voyager Select. On this synth, while oscillator 1 was still a 16' sawtooth, oscillator 2 was outputting a sawtooth set to a fifth above oscillator 1. Filter cutoff, emphasis, and amount of contour were all at about nine o'clock, with the filter envelope attack set to 200 ms, decay to 600 ms, and sustain level to 2. These settings give us a sort of "wow" sound. The loudness contour attack and decay are set to 300 ms and 600 ms, respectively, but the sustain level is zero, because we want a very short-duration sound for this accent.

The main "Billie Jean" bass line uses a simple sawtooth patch with the filter clamped down nearly all the way, accented by a "wow" sound on the first and fourth notes, which are both roots.

MICHAEL JACKSON'S "BEAT IT" GONG

Continuing last month's tribute to Michael Jackson, let's re-create the instantly recognizable intro of "Beat It." Back in '82, Michael and producer Quincy Jones employed a dream team of keyboardists and synth programmers, including heavyweights Greg Phillinganes, Steve Porcaro (of Toto fame), and Michael Boddicker. The famous "Beat It" intro patch was originally a factory demo sound, played by Tom Bähler, from a Synclavier. In addition to high-resolution sampling, the Synclavier had powerful additive and FM digital synthesis, plus multi-track sequencing. Fully loaded systems could cost upwards of $200,000!

Not having a vintage Synclavier around, I let Waldorf's Largo provide the metallic mayhem. You could also try other "digital-sounding" virtual synths, such as the Prophet-VS mode of Arturia's Prophet V, PPG Wave 2.V [*an updated Wave 3.V was released in 2010*], or Image-Line Ogun.

Now play the familiar note sequence:

| G G E E | G G D D |

in octaves, and you'll be showin' 'em how funky and strong is your fight!

1. Start with an initialized patch. In Largo, just click the Edit button above the patch name and select Init Program.

2. Select an appropriate basic waveform. This is trial and error—you want it bright and rich, yet not too heavy on atonal high harmonics (check out my web audio examples for help). I chose "Fuzz Wave" wavetable in Largo.

3. Largo's PPG-style wavetable synthesis lets you sweep through waveforms, either manually or using a mod source, for tonal variation. I manually honed in on a variation by setting the wave number in the top corner of the waveform display to 60.

4. I selected the Chorus 2 wavetable on oscillator two, tuned one octave higher (with wave number 44), and used envelope three to modulate the wave number for timbral motion. Configure the mod routing by clicking the pop-up menu next to the word "Wave," select "Env3," and slide the slider up to a value of 50—Largo displays parameters and associated values at the top of its window as you mouse over them. Click the Envelopes button and set Env3's attack to 89, decay to zero, and sustain and release full up.

5. Experiment with the oscillator volumes in the mixer section; oscillator one gives more fundamental and oscillator two will give more movement and high end.

6. I decided to forgo filtering, but discovered that Largo's filter drive still affects the sound, so crank that guy up to around 51. Bypass the actual filtering by pressing the round "power switch" at the left of the Filter section.

7. In the Envelopes section, set the amp envelope's attack to zero, decay to 85, sustain to 28, and release to 100.

8. It's still pretty bland—time for the mojo! Click the Common button. Set Unisono [sic.] to 6, detune to 18, and spread full up. Now we're triggering six stereo detuned voices with every note. Yeah!

9. I used Largo's high-shelf EQ to kick up the high end a touch, and added some channel bus reverb using Audio Damage's monster new reverb plug-in, EOS.

THOMAS DOLBY'S "WINDPOWER" BASS

Though Thomas Dolby's 1982 smash, "She Blinded Me with Science," was a synth tour de force, those who dug deeper into Dolby's album, *The Golden Age of Wireless*, discovered darker and more serious work, floating in dreamy analog synthscapes, electronic drum thwacks, and percussive, harmonically rich digital synth punctuation. Dolby's use of German PPG synths remains an inspiring example of the uniquely hard, grungy sound of these early digital monsters. Though PPG was best known for the Wave 2.2 and 2.3 models, Dolby used an earlier PPG 340 Wave Computer and 380 Event Generator. This was a rare and finicky keyboard/rack/computer setup originally designed for space-rockers Tangerine Dream. Not only did it incorporate PPG's distinctive digital wavetable synthesis, but the Event Generator was a digital sequencer that Dolby used to trigger drums.

Here we'll use Waldorf's PPG Wave 2.V plug-in to replicate the digital bass patch made famous in the song "Windpower." If you don't have Wave 2.V, you can experiment with other wavetable-style soft synths, or get Wave 2.V as part of the Waldorf Edition package—it streets for a very affordable $100 these days.

That's it. Switch off the mind let the PPG decide! Listen to audio samples at keyboardmag.com and download the "Windpower" patch for Waldorf's PPG Wave 2.V soft synth at celebutantemusic.com/keybmag.

1. The most important factor is selecting the correct wavetable. On PPG synths as well as most Waldorf instruments, a wavetable contains 63 waves. You can play just one wave, or use envelopes or LFOs to sweep through the wavetable, creating the PPG's trademark timbral motion. Wavetables are selected in Wave 2.V by clicking the Digi button on the right; I chose wavetable 13 for its bright tonality.

2. Next we'll set the filter. This patch uses filter modulation from envelope one to make the sound start bright and quickly get darker. Turn the cutoff and emphasis knobs down to about 4. Beneath the filter, turn the Env1 VCF knob to 37—this lets envelope one affect the filter cutoff. Now set ADSR envelope one's attack to zero, decay to 30, sustain to 16, and release to about 19. (Hovering over knobs shows control values on the faux LCD screen.)

3. ADSR envelope two controls volume. Set its controls the same as ADSR 1, and dial the Env2 VCA knob in the Modifiers Control section all the way up. This affects how much influence the envelope has on volume.

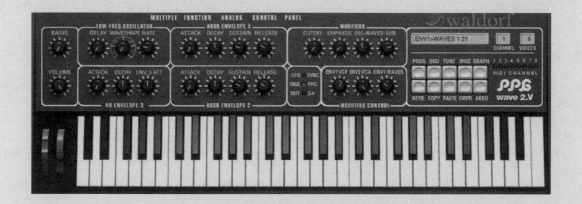

4. Though Wave 2.V isn't a multi-oscillator synth in the traditional sense, you select a main wave and a secondary wave from the master wavetable using the Osc and Sub Waves knobs in the Modifiers section. I set the Osc waves to zero (the first wave in the table) and the Sub wave to 48. Experiment with these for lots of timbral flavors!

5. Now to match the "Windpower" tremolo. I used some LFO modulation routed to the filter. Enable filter mod routing by clicking the Mod button on the right, and set Mod>Filter to on. Click Mod again to get back. In the Low Freq Osc section on the left, set delay at zero, waveshape to triangle, and rate at 16. Now turn the mod wheel at the left of the keyboard up to 14.

6. Now for the signature sound. In the Modifiers Control section, set the Env Waves knob to 21. This makes envelope one sweep through the waves in the wavetable, beginning at the wave we'd selected.

7. For a little widening, insert a quick stereo delay on the PPG's instrument channel in your DAW.

Novation instruments often include the Excite Pack software CD—many include a version of PPG Wave 2.V.

DAFT PUNK'S "DA FUNK"

In 1997, French synth-house duo Daft Punk burst onto the dance scene with the infectiously hooky four-on-the-floor jam "Da Funk." It's such a simple tune that it could almost be a nursery rhyme if it weren't for the radically distorted synth lead drilling its way through the entire track. It's tough to say what synth originally produced it, because the sound is dominated by resonance and distortion, so we'll nail this sound in the soft synth world.

We'll also make it easy for you to get in on the fun by using the cool freeware synth Automat from Alphakanal. I have to admit, I'm pretty blown away by Automat—with three oscillators, dual filters with multiple modes, and built-in effects, this slick little synth can easily hold its own with the paid-for synths you often see me using in this column. Get it at blog.alphakanal.de.

Make sure to play around with the filter cutoff and envelope amount to see how minor tweaks radically affect the tonality of the distortion.

Listen to audio samples of the "Da Funk" patch for Alphakanal Automat at keyboardmag.com, and download this patch at celebutantemusic.com/keybmag.

Step 1. See that little green number 5 under the Pulse Width knob? That's the LFO routed to modulate the oscillator pulse width. You can set the mod depth by holding down the Apple key and click/dragging on the number 5 on a Mac.

Step 2. Set your LFO to a triangle wave, medium speed, and then experiment with the intensity.

1. At its most basic level, this patch consists of two sawtooth waves tuned a perfect fourth apart, so select saw waves for oscillators one and two.

2. Using the coarse oscillator tuning control on oscillator 2, tune it up a perfect fourth (five half steps) from oscillator one.

3. Make sure the volume of each oscillator is fully up in the mixer section directly to the right of the oscillator bank. You can leave oscillator three off by setting its wave to off, or by turning down its volume in the mixer section.

4. Now we'll set the filter. Automat has two filters; oscillator 1 routes to filter one, oscillator two to filter two. Since we want the same filter settings for both oscillators, Automat includes a little "dash" between the two filters. Click it to lock the two filters' controls together.

5. Set the filter type to BP2, which is a two-pole band-pass. Be sure to experiment with the different filter settings later—they all sound great!

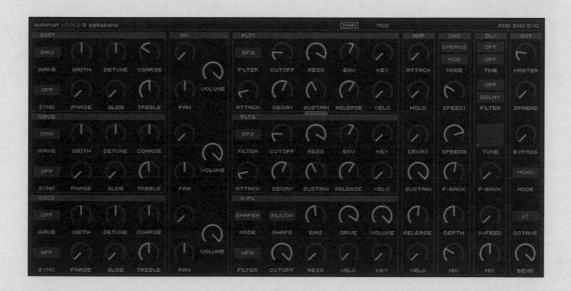

6. Set filter cutoff to nine o'clock, resonance almost full up, envelope amount at about one o'clock, and the filter envelope controls at the following "o'clock" values: attack at eight, decay at one, sustain at eleven, and release at one. See the screenshot for precise values.

7. Moving on to the amp section, simply set sustain full up and release halfway up; everything else can stay at zero.

8. Now we'll use the shaper/filter section (labeled "S-FL" on Automat's panel) to grunge it up. You can experiment with settings, but I set the mode to "shaper," shape to "silicon," bias halfway up, drive almost all the way up, and volume all the way up. Dirty!

9. Select "chorus" from the pop-up menu in the CHO section and dial to taste; try not to go too nuts. Note that my mix control is only about one quarter of the way up.

10. Finally, set the keyboard mode (a drop-down menu all the way to the right) to mono. I also knocked the master transpose down an octave to C1.

EDDY GRANT'S
"ELECTRIC AVENUE"

"Electric Avenue" was one of the biggest MTV hits of the '80s, and still gets crowds bumping on the dance floor. Recently I had to re-create its synth parts for a cover band's backing track. Listening, I realized the trademark "engine-rev" sound wasn't a synth, but actually a delay effect feedback.

Delays "store" incoming sounds and replay them at a settable later time. To get repeats, some of the delayed signal is fed back into the input. If the feedback is high enough, the delay will self-oscillate, like how a mike feeds back when pointed at a speaker. This can turn into something that sounds nothing like the original input. By adjusting the delay time, you can "play" the pitch of this monster noise. This is what's behind the "Electric Avenue" motorcycle rev.

Be careful when cranking up feedback with hardware or software delays! Volume can get out of control and blow speakers, amps, and ears, so turn the master volume down for safety.

1. Any delay will work, but different types have different tones. "Electric Avenue" sounds like an '80s analog "bucket brigade" delay. For this example, I used my Electro-Harmonix Stereo Poly Chorus re-issue. Though it's called a chorus, under the hood it's a short analog delay, and makes great roaring sounds—and lots of other watery weirdness! You can use newer digital delays, but old-school analog and tape delays typically have the tastiest feedback.

2. Here's the weird part. It doesn't matter too much what your initial input sound is, because the delay's own feedback tonality is so dominant. Try a quick, bright synth bass; anything brief with a wide range of harmonics should be fine.

3. Set the delay time close to maximum and the repeats about halfway up. Play a note. Now try cranking the feedback almost all the way (again, watch the volume). Once it's feeding back without you holding a note, play with the delay time knob. This should get you into "engine revving" territory.

4. It takes a little time for the feedback loop to bloom harmonically. Because I wanted to record many passes of revving sounds without playing a note and starting over every time, I left the delay in infinite feedback and improvised a gate so I could turn the sound on and off by playing keys on my modular synth. I fed the pedal output to the synth's VCA and controlled it with a simple on-off envelope triggered by the keyboard. Now I could play the keyboard with my left hand and twist the delay time knob with my right.

5. You can do the same in a DAW by setting up a simple synth with a delay insert effect, followed by a noise gate with a side-chain input. The main channel would use a synth with a brief tone for the delay input. On a second track, insert a synth with any simple on/off sound (such as an organ) and select its output as the input for the noise gate's side chain. Play a note on the first synth and crank the feedback. At

first, bypass the gate so you can hear the delay feed back. Now un-bypass the gate, switch to the second synth, and use it to "play" the effected sound. Listen to audio samples at keyboardmag.com, and download an Apple Logic file set up with the "Electric Avenue" delay effect at celebutantemusic.com/keybmag.

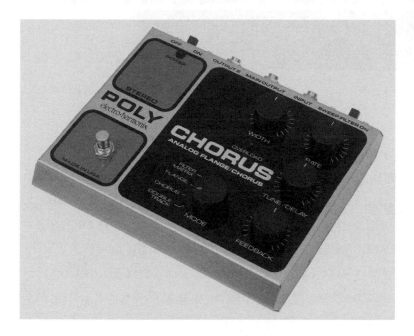

WHAT DELAY TO USE?
I used an Electro-Harmonix Stereo Poly Chorus; their Memory Man models sound great too. Other cool stomps include the Roland RE-20 Space Echo, Moogerfooger Analog Delay, and MXR Carbon Copy. In the computer world, try Tape Delay in Apple Logic or Filter Delay in Ableton Live. If you have a Universal Audio UAD card, the Roland Space Echo plug-in is killer.

LADY GAGA'S "POKER FACE" BASS LINE

FEBRUARY 2010

Lady Gaga stormed the charts last year with "Poker Face," produced and programmed by studio ace RedOne. In our interview in the Oct. '09 issue, he confessed to being a big user of the soft synths included with Apple Logic Pro, so we'll tackle this tune's massive, robotic bass riff using Logic's ES2 synth. If you're not using Logic, you can use any virtual or real analog synth you like, but use one with at least two oscillators and/or a unison mode, because this is a huge patch!

Step 1. Start with big, chewy oscillators. Oscillator one is set to square wave, oscillator two is a sawtooth, and oscillator three is set up for pulse width modulation (see next step). Oscillator one is tuned -24 steps (two octaves down), and oscillator two and three are tuned to -12, putting them an octave above oscillator one. Oscillators two and three are also tuned up and down 10 cents, respectively, for some natural chorusing.

Step 2. Oscillator three is set up for pulse width modulation. PWM lets you affect the width of a pulse wave using a modulation source to add timbral and pitch animation. Here I've set LFO2 to a triangle wave at 2.0 Hz, and have it modulating the pulse width of oscillator three's waveform.

Step 3. Set the mix level of the three oscillators to taste using the triangular mix grid. I pulled it toward oscillators two and three for a more "hyped" sound.

Step 4. Filter settings are simple. Move the Blend slider all the way to right so only filter two is used. Click the 24 dB (per octave, the filter mode) and Fat buttons. Cutoff is all the way open, and resonance is up just a bit to add a bit of high frequency fizz.

Step 5. The volume envelope has the A and D sliders (attack and decay) at zero, S (sustain) full up, and R (release) at 160 ms.

Step 6. In the voice assign section, click the Mono (one note a time) and Unison buttons. I set the Voices parameter to four—hitting each key actually triggers four notes that ES2 automatically detunes and pans across the stereo image. Since this is a three—oscillator patch, that means each note plays 12 oscillators! You can define how much the unison notes are detuned from each other using the Analog knob at the far left of ES2's control panel. I set it to 0.459—pretty seasick!

Step 7. Here's the note pattern for the "Poker Face" bass line.

Hear step-by-step audio examples for this story at keyboardmag.com/How-To and download the "Poker Face" ES2 patch at celebutantemusic.com/keybmag.

SCANDAL'S "GOODBYE TO YOU"

I f you were an early-MTV-generation teen, you probably have the image of singer Patty Smyth's stockinged leg etched into your brain, thanks to Scandal's giddy "Goodbye to You" video. You probably also remember the groovy organ-esque synth solo. Though the video shows keyboardist Benjy King rockin' a rare Digital Keyboards Synergy synth, in reality it's Paul Shaffer manning an Oberheim OB-Xa. Paul has always been a big combo organ fan (he was often photographed playing a Vox Continental), so it's no surprise that he used his Oberheim to cop a cheesy '60s organ feel for "Goodbye to You."

Getting into the Oberheim spirit of things, let's take Sonic Projects OP-X virtual polysynth for a spin—check it out at sonicprojects.ch. You'll need Native Instruments' Reaktor to use it on a Mac, but it's a standard VST plug-in for PC users. Otherwise, you can create this patch on most two-oscillator virtual analog instruments.

Now just add a little stereo chorus and reverb in your DAW's mixer to sweeten the signal. Listen to audio samples and download the patch for Sonic Projects OP-X at keyboardmag.com or celebutantemusic. com/keybmag.

1. Set both oscillators to sawtooth waves. I'd usually use square waves for transistor organ tones, but saws sounded closer in this instance.

2. Set oscillator two's pitch interval two octaves above oscillator one. Detune the oscillators a tiny bit. The detune knob is on the left in OP-X's Control section.

3. Open the filter cutoff frequency all the way.

4. Set the filter resonance to about 25 percent—just enough to thin the tone a bit and make it less "synthy."

5. If you're using OP-X, turn on the Half and Full buttons for oscillator two (but not for noise), located in the Filter section—these emulate an original Oberheim's primitive mixer. On other synths, set the volumes of each oscillator equally in the mixer section.

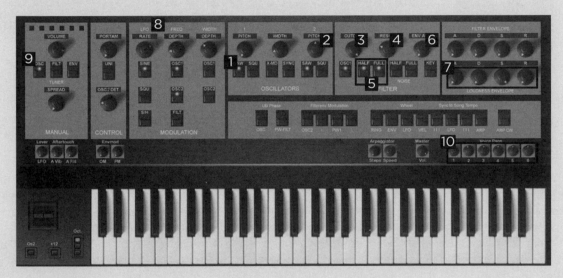

6. Leave the filter envelope amount at zero.

7. Set the loudness envelope to a simple on/off organ shape: everything at zero except for sustain, which is full up.

8. We'll need some '60s vibrato, so set the LFO to a sine wave and the rate relatively fast. In OP-X, make sure the Osc1 and Osc2 buttons in the Modulation section are lit. Now set the depth around a quarter step (in musical pitch terms) either up or down. The secret is to make the vibrato fast and deep without going so far that it sounds like a synthesizer.

9. In OP-X, make sure the Osc button in the Tuner section is clicked; otherwise, pitch will be a little sketchy.

10. Dial all the voice pan knobs on the right of the panel to center.

THE WHO'S "BABA O'RILEY"

The pulsating intro to "Baba O'Riley" ranks among the most instantly recognizable sound bites in rock history. Though many believe it sprung from one of Pete Townshend's massive ARP synthesizers, it was actually a Lowrey Berkshire home organ. Its repeat function added a sixteenth-note pulse to held notes—a gimmick for imitating mandolins and marimbas. With multitracking and clever note phrasing, Townshend made this sound like the future of music.

We'll re-create the "Baba" intro in Apple Logic's ES2. The track has two parts: the basic root-fifth-octave figure, and the additional note flourishes, both using the same patch. You can do it on many virtual analog synths, with one condition: The synth must have a low frequency oscillator (LFO) that retriggers with each key press, as opposed to a common, free-running LFO. Why? Most of the flourishes Pete plays are two held notes struck a 32nd-note apart, creating a "bouncing" auditory illusion as one note plays and the other is silenced. If two notes struck at different times pulse in perfect sync, the "Baba" patch won't sound right; you want independent pulsing for each note. On synths that let you select poly or mono LFO modes, use poly.

As to effects, I added an EQ with 4 dB of low cut at 72 Hz, 7 dB of boost at 2150 Hz, and a high shelf cut of 8.5 dB at 4400 Hz for a '70s tape sound. Logic's GoldVerb on a bus provided small-room ambience. I also panned the main sound left and the reverb right.

Now duplicate the channel strip on two DAW tracks. Set tempo around 117 bpm, and record and quantize the F-C-F-C figure on the first track. Let this play in loop mode while improvising flourishes in the key of F on the second track. It's hard to describe, but you'll instantly hear when you have it right.

1. Set two oscillators (oscillators two and three, in this case) to thin pulse waves for an organ-like sound.

2. Tune the oscillators an octave apart.

3. Detune them by one cent.

4. Mix their volumes equally; in ES2, place the dot equidistant between the two oscillators on the triangle grid.

5. Use a band-pass filter for a mid-rangey tone with few extreme highs or lows, and add some resonance.

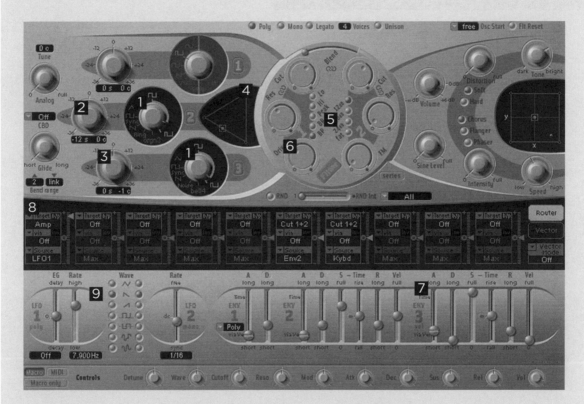

6. Turn up ES2's Drive knob for more lo-fi vibe. Leave filter envelope settings off.

7. Set the volume envelope as follows: attack at 10 ms, decay at zero, sustain at full, and release at 12 ms.

8. To get the sixteenth-note pulse, in ES2's first modulation slot, set Target to Amp and Source to LFO1, and move the green Amount slider up to almost full. (If your synth doesn't have an amp or VCA mod destination, you can modulate a low-pass filter whose cutoff frequency is set to zero instead.)

9. Set LFO1's rate to 7.9 Hz and the waveform to a downward saw. Now held notes will pulse.

DURAN DURAN'S "HUNGRY LIKE THE WOLF"

Duran Duran were the poster children of the 80's with a string of MTV-era hits that still rock the clubs today. Nick Rhodes's mix of swirling atmospherics and percolating arpeggios went a long way toward establishing the band's hit-making sound. Let's make the signature arpeggio of "Hungry Like the Wolf," originally played on a Roland Jupiter-8 and re-created here using Arturia's Jupiter-8V soft synth. Almost any virtual analog synth will work, as long as it has an arpeggiator with a "random" note order setting.

Step 1. We'll use two oscillators, both set to square waves. Oscillators should be tuned in unison with the fine-tune knob at about one o' clock—enough so a bit of chorusing happens.

Step 2. The Source Mix knob should be smack in the middle for an equal blend of each oscillator.

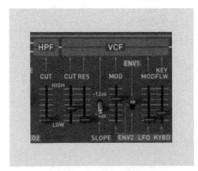

Step 3. The high-pass filter (HPF) isn't used, so turn its slider off. Cutoff is mostly closed down, because we'll use the filter envelope to control the frequency. Set the cutoff to 322 Hz, and cutoff envelope mod amount to .667 (just over halfway). Make sure the switch next to the mod slider is set to ENV1; this lets ENV1 modulate the cutoff frequency while ENV2 affects amplitude. Set the resonance at zero, and add a little key follow to brighten higher notes.

Step 4. Now set ENV1 as shown: A = zero, D = 234 ms, S = zero, and R = 1324 ms

Step 5. ENV2 shapes the amplitude of the sound. A = zero, D = 4761 ms, S = zero, and R = 2 556 ms. These may seem like long times for such a quick sound, but the sound actually does ring for a bit, though the release phase is muted by the rapid filter envelope.

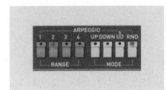

Step 6. Now for the fun part. Set the arpeggiator to random mode (RND) and the range to two octaves. Lock up the timing by setting your host's tempo around 127 bpm, and set the arpeggio rate to sixteenth notes. Set the neighboring sync switch to external—this locks the arpeggiator to your host's MIDI clock. Add a little reverb, hold down some E and D major triads, and you'll be off and running! Listen to audio samples at keyboard-mag.com, and download the patch for Arturia Jupiter 8V at celebutantemusic.com/keybmag.

Arturia's Jupiter 8-V version 2 was released in February 2010.

ROBERT PALMER'S
"ADDICTED TO LOVE"

JUNE 2010

Who could forget the suit-and-tie-clad Robert Palmer surrounded by a "band" of five vapid models obviously only pretending to play? Considering the small fortunes spent on videos then, "Addicted to Love" was cheap, simple, and used the oldest trick in the book: hot girls in slinky dresses. It didn't hurt that "Addicted" was a seriously catchy tune featuring big 'n' brassy synth stabs. This month we'll create our own beefy analog stabs on hardware and software synths: the Alesis Ion and Native Instruments' Massive. You can make this patch on just about any analog or virtual analog synth that has two (or better, three) oscillators. Follow the steps and you too will be "Addicted to Love."

Step 1. Set all available oscillators to pulse waves.

Step 2. Set the oscillators an octave apart; if you have three oscillators, put two at the same pitch and the third an octave up. Detune all oscillators enough to hear some chorusing, but not enough to sound audibly out of tune.

Step 3. For tonal motion, route an envelope generator (usually the one that controls the filter) to control the pulse width of the oscillator waves. Set attack around 100 ms, decay at 300 ms, sustain to medium, and release off. These don't need to be exact, so don't worry if your synth doesn't show times.

Step 4. Using a low-pass filter, set the cutoff frequency relatively low, then turn up the envelope amount knob so that the envelope you set in step 3 controls the cutoff. You may need to experiment, but we want it to sound like a brass section.

Step 5. Set the volume envelope similar to the filter: attack around 100 ms, decay at 300 ms, sustain full up, and release off. Make sure the attack isn't too fast, as it takes time to blow air through a real horn.

Step 6. Add a thick, juicy chorus effect, either from the synth itself or as an insert effect in your DAW's channel strip.

Listen to audio samples at keyboardmag.com and download the "Addicted" patch for Native Instruments' Massive at celebutantemusic.com/keybmag.

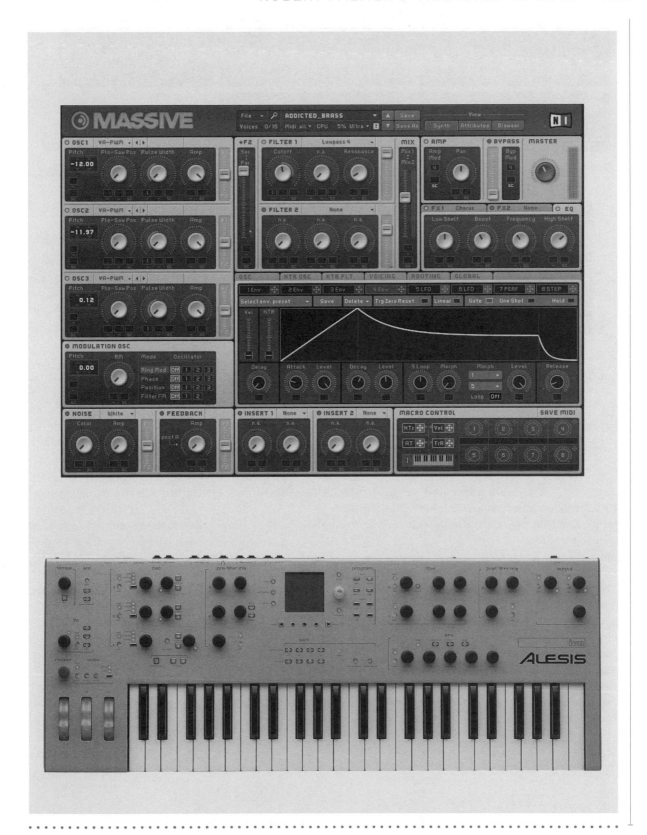

HERBIE HANCOCK'S "CHAMELEON"

Herbie Hancock's music has traversed many paths over the years, but in the early '70s, the album *Head Hunters* set the standard for jazz-funk fusion. Using a combination of Clavinet, Rhodes electric piano, and ARP synth, *Head Hunters* also featured innovative tones, because back in '73, funky Clav lines and fat, resonant synth bass were far from clichéd. This month, we'll recapture the funky and unmistakable ARP Odyssey bass sound used in the intro of "Chameleon." I used GForce Oddity, a faithful virtual re-creation of the Odyssey. Prodyssey for Use Audio's Plugiator tabletop synth is also spot-on, but any analog-style monosynth will work great.

Step 1. We'll use just one oscillator, set to a sawtooth wave. If you're using Oddity, select "saw" in the filter mixer section and turn up the blue VCO1 slider.

Step 2. Set the VCF cutoff frequency very low—almost off—then set resonance to around the middle of its range.

Step 3. Route an envelope generator to control the filter cutoff and turn it up about 75 percent. On Oddity, select "ADSR" using the switch beneath the red filter mod slider in the filter mixer section.

Step 4. Set the ADSR controls: attack at zero, medium decay, low sustain, and medium release. If you're using a synth with separate envelopes for filter and amplitude, set them identically.

Step 5. Add distortion! I found it easier to match Herbie's sound with an amp simulator, as opposed to a stomp-box-style distortion. The "Small Tweed Combo" model in Logic's Amp Designer plug-in really hit the spot. I pumped up the gain and mids a hair, and easily nailed the tone.

Step 6. The amp modeling will really change the tone, so now we'll fine-tune. Tweak the filter cutoff, resonance, and filter mod controls (as well as envelope decay and release) to really get things dialed in. Listen to audio samples at keyboardmag.com, and download the "Chameleon" patch for GForce Oddity at celebutantemusic.com/keybmag.

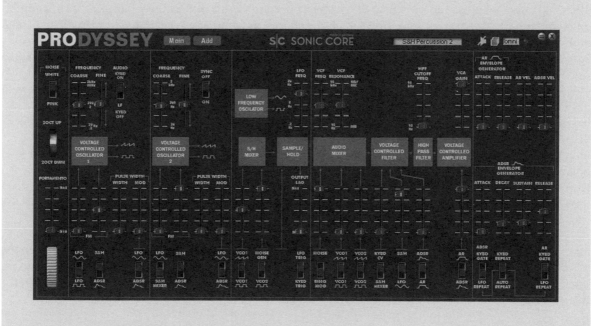

ERASURE'S "A LITTLE RESPECT"

Vince Clarke has cemented his place as a legend of synth pop. In the '80s, he penned numerous hits with Depeche Mode prior to forming smash duo Yaz with singer Alison Moyet. Yaz disbanded after just two albums, but Vince returned with singer Andy Bell in 1986 to form Erasure, and they've released 13 albums since. Full of Vince's bubbly synth stylings, "A Little Respect" is perhaps their best-known track. Let's examine the synth-and-piano chordal figure that drives the track. I used Arturia's Prophet-V; a real analog synth such as a Prophet '08 would also rule.

Step 1. Set up a piano sound in your DAW. It doesn't need to have a big memory footprint, as a medium-quality piano will do. Add compression and stereo chorus, as well as an EQ with bass rolled off and some high-shelf boost.

Step 2. Turn to your analog or virtual analog synth and set both oscillators to a pulse wave at the same pitch. Detune them by a couple of cents. Set the waveform to pulse wave for both oscillators.

Step 3. Set the low-frequency oscillator (LFO) to a triangle wave at a rate of about 5 Hz, and route it to both oscillators' pulse width. Set the modulation depth around 75 percent. Things should be pretty warbly here—the straight piano sound you'll layer in tends to un-warble the overall tone.

Step 4. Set both oscillators to full volume in the oscillator mix section.

Step 5. Set filter cutoff about 75 percent open, resonance off, envelope amount to 50 percent, and keyboard tracking to full.

Step 6. By turning up the envelope amount knob, the filter cutoff will be lightly controlled by the envelope generator. Set the filter attack at 20 ms, decay at 300 ms, sustain at 50 percent, and release at 300 ms—these values don't have to be exact. Duplicate these settings for the volume envelope.

Now program and quantize the chords in your sequencer, and make sure to copy the sequence for the piano and synth sounds. It's all simple triads, mostly in C, so it should be pretty easy to pay a little respect to Mr. Clarke. Listen to audio samples at keyboardmag.com and download the "Respect" patch for Arturia Prophet-V at celebutantemusic.com/keybmag.

MADONNA'S "LUCKY STAR"

Most folks think of '80s-vintage Madonna and remember the hair, rubber bracelets, and attire that spawned a generation of dress-alikes. Listen to the Material Girl's early hits, though, and you'll find some pretty sweet vintage synth work. This month we'll break down the swirling, arpeggiated intro of "Lucky Star." You can create the patch on just about any two-oscillator virtual or real analog synth, but you'll certainly need to sequence it! I used AlphaKanal's nifty free soft synth Automat for Mac OS X.

Step 1. Select a pulse wave for oscillator 1. Set it to a medium width using the pulse width control.

Step 2. Select a sawtooth wave for oscillator 2. Tune it to the same octave as oscillator 1, but detune a couple of cents from oscillator 1 for subtle chorusing. Set the mix of both oscillators equally.

Step 3. Select a 24-dB-per-octave (or four-pole) low-pass filter (LP4 in Automat) and set the cutoff frequency fully open. Set the resonance to 50 percent to thin the sound out. Filter envelope amount and key tracking can be left at zero.

Step 4. Set the amplitude envelope as follows: attack at zero, decay at 10 percent, and sustain and release both at zero. You'll need to fine-tune the decay amount, but this is best done after the note sequence is programmed.

Step 5. Using a bus send effect or insert, add a quick single sixteenth-note delay. (This comes out to 127 ms at "Lucky Star's tempo of 118 bpm.) Add a large hall reverb with about three seconds of decay using a stereo send to a stereo bus. Finally, add some low-shelf EQ to reduce clickiness and a slow panner to replicate the stereo movement.

Step 6. Program the note sequence—an arpeggiated A sus chord playing 32nd notes, ascending four octaves then descending in groups of three:

A D E | D E A | E A D | etc.

I recommend programming in half-time with a click, then quantizing. Listen to audio samples at keyboardmag.com and download the "Lucky Star" patch AlphaKanal Automat at celebutantemusic.com/keybmag.

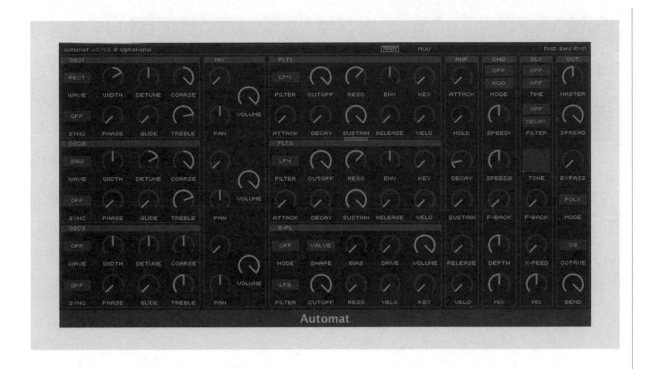

FIVE LEGENDARY MINIMOOG SOUNDS

Without a doubt, the Minimoog is *the* classic analog synth, so much that early recordings often attributed any synth simply as "Moog" on album sleeve credits. The progressive-rock and jazz-fusion movements pushed the Mini into the spotlight during the '70s. Let's check out some of the Mini's patches that made it famous, with patch diagrams from today's Minimoog Voyager Old School. These translate to the "regular" Voyager (though the modulation section is configured somewhat differently), and soft synth imitations equally well.

A couple of general notes: No two analog synths are alike, so if the oscillator tuning, filter settings, or envelope of a patch doesn't sound quite right to you, experiment with very small knob movements. Also, we've left the second modulation bus blank, as it's not critical to any of these patches. You could use it to add more performance control, e.g., opening up the filter a bit when you apply aftertouch.

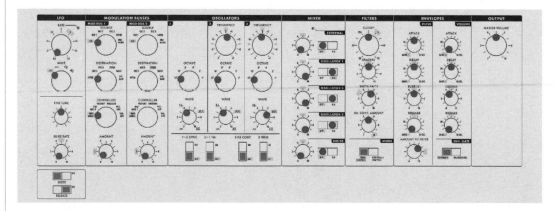

1. SUPER FUNKY BASS
Here's the funky, squirty bass patch used in the Bee Gees' "Jive Talkin'" and countless disco classics. We're using all three oscillators with the first two set to sawtooth waves, and the third set to a square wave for thickness. The oscillators are detuned very slightly: +1 cent for oscillator one, and -1 for oscillator three. Filter cutoff is 50 percent open and resonance is about 60 percent of maximum.

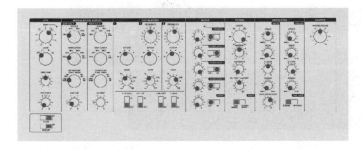

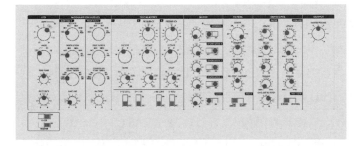

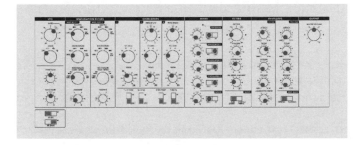

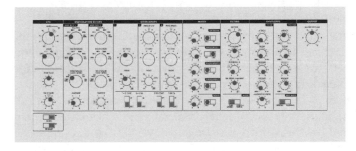

2. RUSH'S "TOM SAWYER" LEAD

One of the most recognizable synth leads ever. The secret to this patch is two sawtooth oscillators just barely detuned from each other. You'll need to tweak oscillator two's Fine-Tune knob until the oscillators almost sync—check out the online audio examples for reference. Another critical aspect: just a little bit of glide, i.e., a fast rate. (Clockwise = slower on the Voyager's glide knob.)

3. ELP'S "LUCKY MAN" LEAD

The other most recognizable synth lead! Keith Emerson sets all three oscillators to slightly detuned square waves with the filter wide open and a generous amount of glide. Add some reverb for flavor, and go nuts with the octave and resonance knobs at the end.

4. WAKEMAN WAH

Rick Wakeman really put the classic ladder filter to use in his "Catherine of Aragon" from "The Six Wives of Henry VIII." Three slightly detuned saw oscillators, a whole lot of filter resonance, and a very slow filter envelope are the keys to this patch.

5. PSEUDO-THEREMIN

As heard in the Portishead track "Humming" from "Roseland NYC Live," this simple one-oscillator sawtooth patch with heavy vibrato from the LFO, along with a fairly slow glide, evokes '50s sci-fi shows. This patch sounds great with spring reverb emulation. Listen to audio samples at keyboardmag.com or celebutantemusic.com/keybmag.

KARN FROM KEITH, KATE FROM RICK

As this month's *Keyboard* pays tribute to Keith Emerson, we'll cook up one classic Moog patch from him, then another from the only other rock keyboard hero people speak of in the same breath: Rick Wakeman of Yes. We begin with the instantly recognizable intro patch from ELP's "Karn Evil 9: 1st Impression, Pt. 2." I used Arturia's Moog Modular V, a virtual Moog modular emulator.

Step 1. Amble up to your monstrous Moog modular, or perhaps a plug-in equivalent, and set two or three oscillators to sawtooth waves in unison, then detune them enough to achieve a thick chorusing effect.

Step 2. Route the oscillator outputs to filter 1, then route its output to the VCA in jack at the bottom right corner of envelope 1.

Step 3. Set the filter cutoff relatively low, and emphasis (resonance) just high enough so that a secondary "ringing" is heard.

Step 4. Set the amplitude envelope controls for a long attack, zero decay, full sustain, and long release. This isn't crucial, just make sure the sustain is up.

Step 5. Now for the secret sauce: Modulate the filter cutoff frequency with a low-frequency oscillator

(LFO) set to a sample-and-hold waveform. Dependent upon LFO rate, this chooses a random value and keeps it there for a fixed time before moving on to another value. Set LFO frequency to about 9.5 Hz. Make sure the "Manual" knob is full up in the LFO section, then connect a cable from the sample-and-hold waveform output in the VC LFO module (the one at far right with a squiggly line above it) to the filter cutoff modulation input, then turn up the mod amount to about 0.4068 using the "ring" control on the input jack.

Step 6. Tweak the cutoff frequency and emphasis controls to dial in the sound.

Step 7. For the full stereo effect, pan the sound slightly to the left in your DAW, then use a bus send reverb set to a vintage spring or plate, and pan that slightly to the right.

Rick Wakeman's solo masterpiece *The Six Wives of Henry VIII* is full of screaming Minimoog solos, but I've chosen one of the more unique patches, heard around the 4:00 mark on "Catherine Parr." It's a lead with a pronounced, slow-resonating filter sweep that doesn't follow individual notes. This is because stock Minimoogs only retrigger the filter envelopes if all notes have been released; when the envelopes are set to slow times, they continue to run when notes are fingered legato. I used Arturia Minimoog V to create the patch.

Step 1. Set all three oscillators to sawtooth waves. Set oscillators one and two at 16', and oscillator three at 8', then detune them for a gentle chorus effect.

Step 2. Make sure all three oscillator on/off switches are on in the mixer and set their volumes equally.

Step 3. Set filter cutoff around 200 Hz, and Emphasis (resonance) all the way up—turn down your speakers prior to doing this! Set "Amount of Contour" halfway up, attack at 10 ms, decay around 1700 ms, and sustain around 2.

Step 4. Now set the Loudness Contour (volume envelope): attack about 300 ms, decay around 800 ms, and sustain at full.

Step 5. In the control section to the left of the keyboard, make sure the Glide, Decay, and Legato switches are all on, and turn the glide knob up about halfway.

Step 6. Add some long, dark spring or hall reverb with an insert or bus effect for atmosphere.

When playing this patch, notice how the resonance sweeps slowly over the notes when playing legato. It's like getting two sounds in one!

THOMAS DOLBY'S "CLOUD BURST AT SHINGLE STREET"

If you're a regular "Steal This Sound" reader, you know that we've covered Mr. Dolby's imaginative synth programming before—there's lots of great stuff there! This month, we'll break down the beautiful chord pulses of "Cloudburst at Shingle Street" from his first full-length album, *The Golden Age of Wireless*. We'll use Native Instruments' Massive, but other synths will work as long they include some "digital-sounding" single-cycle waves.

Step 1. Start with two oscillators an octave apart and detune them about 15 cents for chorusing. I used the "Additiv 1" wave for both oscillators to replicate the original track's PPG digital synth. Set both oscillators at equal volume.

Step 2. Using a low-pass filter, set the cutoff frequency at about 50 percent, then route an envelope to control the cutoff. Do this in Massive by dragging the "1Env" icon to one of the empty squares beneath the Cutoff knob. Set the modulation amount by command-clicking then dragging—you'll see a blue band around the Cutoff knob's circumference. Drag this band so it spans from 12 o'clock to about three o'clock. Turn the resonance up to around 20 percent.

Step 3. Click the icon for envelope 1 ("1Env"), used to control filter cutoff frequency. Set attack to zero, decay and level at 50 percent, and release at 60 percent.

Step 4. Click the icon for envelope 4 ("4Env"), used to control amplitude. Set attack to zero, decay and level at 40 percent, and release at 50 percent.

Step 5. Add effects. I used a fair amount of Massive's "Chorus Ensemble" followed by "Delay Synced." Set the delay very wet, with a lot of feedback—about a dozen audible repeats. Delay time should be eighth notes at about 143 bpm (around 210 ms).

Step 6. Add a channel strip EQ in your DAW. This may or may not be needed, but Massive's "Additiv 1" oscillator wave needed more piano-like resonance, so I boosted 5 dB at 164 Hz, and brightened it with a high shelf of 10 dB at 3750 Hz.

That should get you pretty close. Try different single-cycle digital waves for different tones—that and the long, pulsing delay will inspire your own tunes in no time! You can download the "Cloudburst" patch for Native Instruments Massive as well as some audio sounds samples at www.keyboardmag.com, or at www.celebutantemusic/keybmag.

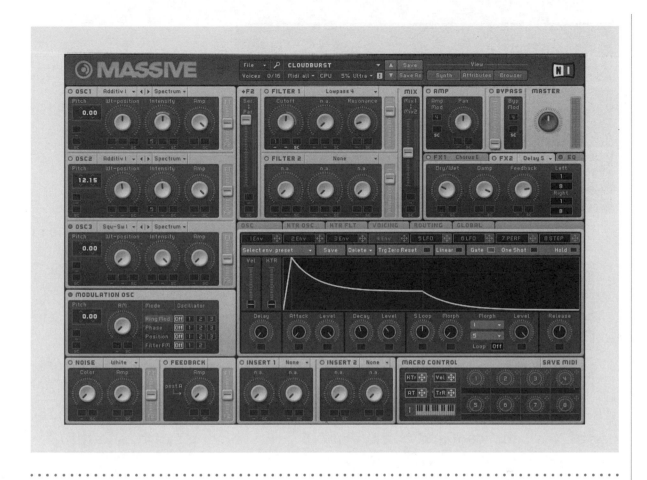

PINK FLOYD'S "WELCOME TO THE MACHINE"

Perhaps unintentionally, Pink Floyd became one of the great innovators of the use of synths in rock. We dissected the frenetic instrumental "On the Run" from *The Dark Side of the Moon* way back in the April '05 issue. This month, we'll look at the throbbing intro of "Welcome to the Machine" from the album *Wish You Were Here*." Originally created using an EMS VCS3 synth, I made use of Xils Labs' cool and quirky PolyKB virtual analog synth, a faithful representation of the extremely rare RSF PolyKobol.

Step 1. We'll need two sawtooth wave oscillators tuned one octave apart and slightly detuned for fatness, so hit PolyKB's Detune button. PolyKB's unusual oscillators allow continuously variable waveforms; I set each waveform knob to between nine and ten o'clock to get standard saw waves. PolyKB also has an odd way of setting oscillator volume: oscillator one has a pair of buttons (I lit up both for maximum volume) and oscillator two has a knob (I turned it all the way up).

Step 2. In addition to our grinding saw waves, we want a good deal of white noise in there. On PolyKB, press both White Noise buttons for maximum volume. On any other synth, turn the noise up to the same level as the oscillators.

Step 3. Moving on to the filter, set the cutoff to about 60 percent open (1500 Hz on PolyKB), and resonance to about 20 percent—just a little bit of wah.

Step 4. The volume envelope is a straight gate shape: attack at zero, decay at zero, sustain full up, and release at zero.

Step 5. The most important aspect of our sound is a triangle-wave LFO slowly modulating the filter's cutoff frequency. On PolyKB, set the LFO wave to triangle and rate to 9.10 (about 4 Hz), dial the LFO1 knob in the Modulations section up to 22 percent, and click the VCF button to its right once, so that only the red (left) LED is lit. You may need to experiment with rate and depth on other synths.

Step 6. Now add a big, lo-fi spring reverb. I used the "LoFi Amp Middle B" setting in Apple Logic's convolution plug-in, Space Designer.

So welcome to the PolyKB machine. Try not to scare the neighbors with that big bass! You can download the "Machine" patch for Xils Labs PolyKB as well as some audio sounds samples at www.keyboardmag.com, or at www.celebutantemusic/keybmag.